T0304957

"*The Science of Channeling* provides the ev
to come out of the closet about their nonlocal consciousness experiences. in
wisdom traditions throughout the world, 'revelation' is an important aspect of
channeling. A beautiful synergy between science and direct experience,
Wahbeh excellently summarizes channeling research and provides accessible
ways for how we can use channeling in our lives every day. A must-have introduction to how our consciousness can transcend time and space."

> —**Deepak Chopra, MD**, founder of The Chopra Foundation;
> world-renowned pioneer in integrative medicine and personal
> transformation; and author of more than ninety books
> translated into more than forty-three languages, including
> numerous *New York Times* bestsellers

"Evolving science reveals a world that is based on our intrinsic unity and connections with one another, in which there are no fundamental separations
between humans in either space or time. For a glimpse of this world, Helané
Wahbeh's *The Science of Channeling* is essential."

> —**Larry Dossey, MD**, author of *One Mind*

"*The Science of Channeling* is a remarkable book. It presents the latest scientific understanding of psychic phenomena from two unique perspectives: The
author is both an experienced scientist who studies these phenomena, and she
is also a natural psychic. Helané Wahbeh describes her personal journey, what
is known and not known about these abilities, and how to cultivate your
distinctive gifts. Highly recommended."

> —**Dean Radin, PhD**, chief scientist at the Institute of
> Noetic Sciences (IONS)

"In this reader-friendly book, Helané Wahbeh tells her readers that they have access to many sources of creativity and well-being—sources that go beyond the conventional notion that people end where their skin ends. After reviewing numerous studies and remarkable case histories, she provides practical suggestions for accessing these sources through such activities as meditation, dreaming, nature walks, and setting intentions. She also advises discernment as not all information gained through 'channeling' can be trusted, much less verified. This book has the potential to change its readers' lives, and contains commonsense exercises that can be transformative as well as entertaining."

> —**Stanley Krippner, PhD**, associated distinguished professor at California Institute of Integral Studies, and coauthor of *Personal Mythology*

"In her newest book, *The Science of Channeling*, Helané Wahbeh has created a seminal work on the confluence of science and spirituality. Her cogent and in-depth exploration of channeling and the clarity of her writing provides the reader with insight into the inner self, the intuitive quality we each possess. Helané's inquisitive nature probes long-held beliefs and societal concepts, giving us a wisdom feast to be read again and again."

> —**Jean Houston**, author of *The Wizard of Us*

"*The Science of Channeling* is an excellent and greatly needed investigation into the reality of channeling and its experiential benefits. It's also a great exemplar of science; to follow the evidence wherever it leads. Its expertly summoned and compelling evidence aligns with the emergence of a new wholistic paradigm of the unified and nonlocal nature of reality, within which such supernormal phenomena are both natural and innate to human consciousness."

> —**Jude Currivan, PhD**, cosmologist, author of *The Cosmic Hologram*, and cofounder of WholeWorld-View

"Helané Wahbeh gently but firmly puts the science of channeling on the map in this brave and beautiful book. But more important than that, the pioneering research and precious wisdom she shares will help every reader learn how to notice, trust, and love what is real beyond their five senses. After reading it, you'll be left in absolutely no doubt that tuning into what is unseen is your key to a deeply fulfilling life."

—**Theresa Cheung**, *Sunday Times* top-ten best-selling author writing about dreams, paranormal, and spiritual and personal growth; with degrees in theology and English from King's College, Cambridge University

"This is one of those books you don't realize was missing until it shows up in your life. Helané Wahbeh takes an informed, sober, and curious look at receiving information across time and space, through non-sensory means. This may be the only book in the world that covers essential topics like discernment regarding channeled information, relation to mental health, and how to use channeling for good—all in one engaging volume."

—**Julia Mossbridge, PhD**, fellow at IONS, and coauthor of *The Premonition Code*

The Science of Channeling

Why You Should Trust Your Intuition & Embrace the Force That Connects Us All

Helané Wahbeh, ND, MCR

New Harbinger Publications, Inc.
Institute of Noetic Sciences

Publisher's Note

Distributed in Canada by Raincoast Books

NEW HARBINGER PUBLICATIONS is a registered trademark of
New Harbinger Publications, Inc.

Noetic Signature is a registered trademark of the Institute of Noetic Sciences

Copyright © 2021 by Helané Wahbeh
        Reveal Press/Institute of Noetic Sciences
        (Reveal Press is an imprint of New Harbinger
        Publications, Inc.)
        www.newharbinger.com

Cover design by Amy Daniel; Acquired by Ryan Buresh;
Edited by Gretel Hakanson

Library of Congress Cataloging-in-Publication Data

Names: Wahbeh, Helané, author.
Title: The science of channeling : why you should trust your intuition and embrace the
    force that connects us all / by Helané Wahbeh.
Description: Oakland, CA : New Harbinger Publications, [2021] | Includes bibliographi-
    cal references.
Identifiers: LCCN 2021009009 | ISBN 9781684037155 (trade paperback)
Subjects: LCSH: Channeling (Spiritualism)
Classification: LCC BF1286 .W28 2021 | DDC 133.9/1--dc23
LC record available at https://lccn.loc.gov/2021009009

Printed in the United States of America

23   22   21

10 9 8 7 6 5 4 3 2 1   First Printing

For Mícheál and Mateen

May children everywhere feel heard, loved, and supported
when they share about their channeling.

Contents

Foreword

In the last few decades, we have witnessed extraordinary expansion in our understanding of the mind-brain relationship and the nature of consciousness. As the brilliant observer of the human psyche, psychologist William James, noted in the early twentieth century: something *more* is required to explain the full range of human experience. Bringing together numerous lines of evidence from many different fields point today's science of consciousness toward a remarkable recognition that we can no longer simply assume extraordinary experiences are some side effect of arrangements of matter in the physical brain. Rather, mind has a fundamental role in determining reality.

This thought revolution has integrated the neuroscience of consciousness (especially the "hard problem" of consciousness, apparently an insurmountable problem for conventional physicalism). Other fields include philosophy of mind, psychology and parapsychology (notably myriad examples of *non-local consciousness*), and the counterintuitive, yet profoundly demonstrated, aspects of quantum physics (specifically *superposition* and *entanglement*).

The book you are holding contributes a rigorous approach to scientifically investigating a human capability known as *channeling*. This catchall term refers to numerous human activities that result from our ability, as sentient beings, to tap into a causal mental layer of the universe—known as *non-local consciousness* in parapsychology. Such abilities include telepathy (mind-to-mind communications), precognition (knowledge of the immediate future), presentiment (emotional and autonomic-nervous-system awareness of the immediate future), clairvoyance (including remote viewing, aura reading, animal communications, and more), and intuition or clairsentience. These aspects of channeling involve acquiring information beyond the purview of conventional physical senses. Forms of channeling also involve our will influencing the world, such as remote influence, distance healing, and psychokinesis.

Collecting channeling experiences is crucial to furthering the revolution in the science of consciousness. The author, Helané Wahbeh, grew up in a family of channelers who nurtured her experience through the richness of sharing techniques and successes. Such robust experiences were natural in her interactions with the world, so she was surprised to find that not everyone believed in their viability. She honed her personal skills through interactions with her trance channeling relatives, and further refined them through an active, regular practice of meditation. Originally trained as a naturopathic healer, she pursued the academic study of mindfulness meditation and acquired a National Institutes of Health (NIH) grant to support her scientific efforts. This work ultimately resulted in her joining the Institute of Noetic Sciences (IONS), a research group founded by astronaut Dr. Edgar Mitchell, who in 1971 had an epiphany aboard the Apollo 14 moon mission while returning to Earth.

Helané Wahbeh realized that working as the research director for IONS might threaten her academic career, because of their exceptional open-mindedness. Tackling very deep and hitherto unsolved problems involving the vast nature of consciousness is not being done by less courageous mainstream scientific investigators. She did not want to spend the rest of her life doing limited research that didn't address the big issues she suspected were scientifically approachable. The result of her collaboration with IONS is this wonderful and informative book.

Research suggests that all humans have channeling capabilities, and that persistent and regular application of proven techniques can help anyone develop these normally latent skills. This book serves as an excellent starting point for such individual work, as well as being a useful guide for more advanced practice. Ever since my near-death experience in 2008, I have come to rely on a regular practice of going within as part of my daily life. Firsthand knowledge of the fundamental nature of mind is available to us all through myriad methods and techniques.

Just as medical science has come to realize the power of the placebo effect as a robust real-world example of the potential for mind-over-matter influence in our health, the scientific community at large is beginning to realize the primacy of consciousness's influence in our lives and reality. This has been well demonstrated in the recent evolution of the science of consciousness, which fully supports the reality of channeling as a useful human capability.

So fasten your seatbelt and prepare for an exciting, informative journey into the greater aspects of human potential revealed in this engaging and practical book.

—Eben Alexander, MD
Neurosurgeon and author of *Proof of Heaven* and *Living in a Mindful Universe*

INTRODUCTION

My Quest for Answers

I am a clinician, academic, and research scientist. Never did I imagine as an academic that I would write a book about the science of channeling. Academia doesn't accept channeling. Thanks to the Institute of Noetic Sciences—where I am director of research—I can pair my passion with my academic training to offer you a message that can change your perceptions about channeling, your abilities, and how you apply it to your life and the collective goals of humanity.

I've hidden my channeling ability most of my life. Apparently, so have many others. People always approach me after talks or send me private emails saying, "Thank you so much. You know, I had this experience that I've never told anyone…" Then they share their secret channeling experience. So many people have channeling experiences but hide them because of taboos in our culture. Taboos are social or religious customs that cause people to block or refuse to discuss a particular practice or topic or refuse to associate with a specific person, place, or thing. The fact that you are reading these words means that you are curious about channeling and are willing to ignore the taboos and explore further.

Perhaps you have had a channeling experience and are confused or fearful about it. If so, this book is meant to say, "No, there is nothing wrong with you, and here is the evidence demonstrating that." Maybe you regularly channel but are frustrated because sharing it doesn't seem possible. Perhaps there haven't been any resources that you can share with others to support your channeling. Now, you can hold up this book and say, "See, other people have these experiences too. In fact, it is actually quite common. Here's what we know about it and how it works."

Maybe you've never had a channeling experience and are curious. For you, this book will provide a general background on what we know today about channeling from a scientific perspective. While this book is not an exhaustive, comprehensive review of all things channeling, you will gain a broad understanding of channeling research by reading it.

If you haven't had a channeling experience but really want to, you will learn and develop your channeling ability. Whatever your motivation is for reading this book, you will find a piece of what you are looking for, or at the least, you'll be guided in the right direction on your path.

An Overview of My Life's Work

I'd like to introduce myself by sharing a bit about my scientific background. I completed my undergraduate degree in anthropology and premedicine at the University of California at Berkeley. I am clinically trained and received my naturopathic doctorate at the National University of Natural Medicine. Naturopathic physicians, or NDs, are trained as primary care physicians and base their practice on six tenets: the body has its own innate ability to heal itself (*vis medicatrix naturae*); treat the root cause of illness (*tolle causam*); first, do no harm (*primum non nocere*); doctor as teacher (*docere*); treat the whole person; and prevention. With this philosophy, NDs use several tools to help people on their path to optimal health. My specialty in private practice was mind-body medicine, including meditation.

I received extensive meditation training, including the Mindfulness-Based Stress Reduction teacher training by Jon Kabat-Zinn and a four-year meditation teacher training with CoreLight, and I developed a strong personal practice. Meditation was one inspiration for transitioning from private practice into clinical research. The benefits of meditation were excellent for my patients and me. I wanted to learn more about how meditation worked and how to use it more effectively to help people.

I completed two postdoctoral research fellowships: one at my medical school and another through the Oregon Center for Complementary and Alternative Medicine in Neurological Disorders and funded by the National Institutes of Health. I received a career development award from the National Institutes of Health in which I obtained a master's in clinical research at Oregon Health and Science University. This grant also funded a five-year study that evaluated mindfulness meditation for combat veterans with post-traumatic stress disorder.

In a decade and a half of academic research, I conducted numerous clinical studies in various populations, including combat veterans with PTSD, stressed older adults, and dementia caregivers. I collected saliva, blood, and urine; and measured pupils, brain waves, heart waves, skin, and temperature. I stressed and relaxed participants and taught them how to meditate. I sat on government grant panels and institutional review boards. I have published on and spoken internationally about my studies on complementary and alternative medicine, mind-body medicine, stress, and post-traumatic stress disorder—and their relationships to physiology, health, and healing.

Through this background and many synchronistic events, I became a staff scientist and then director of research at the Institute of Noetic Sciences. I now have the freedom to scientifically evaluate the channeling phenomenon. Before we delve into the science and relevance of channeling in today's world, I want to give you a broader view of my personal channeling experience. I believe this will provide you with some context for my motivation to study channeling and the lens through which I perceive it.

But, you may wonder, *Shouldn't scientists be completely unbiased? If you believe in it and have experienced it, doesn't that skew your results to what you want to find?* Perhaps, but it also gives me a unique perspective on how to study channeling. Please don't take my word for it; I invite you to read the book and answer that question for yourself. Here are where my footsteps along this journey started.

My Early Encounters with Channeling

You wouldn't know from my academic biography that I come from a long line of trance channelers. You also wouldn't know that every single member of my mother's family has channeling abilities. My grandmother surprised everyone by going into a trance at fifteen years old. My grandmother was what some might call a trance channeler. Trance channelers go into trancelike states and believe that they use their bodies as a "vehicle" for a nonphysical "being" to incorporate into and communicate directly via speaking, writing, or movement. My grandmother could withdraw the control of her body and allow another "being" to control it. She was not conscious of what was happening with her body when in a trance. She described it as stepping aside and going to sleep within herself while another "being" took her spirit's place; it took over her voice and her movements. And even though she was "sleeping," she felt totally safe. My mother is also a trance channeler. My uncle was tested for psychokinetic skills at John F. Kennedy University and channeled a book through automatic writing.[1] Automatic writing is a type of channeling where a person handwrites meaningful statements, but without the writer consciously premeditating the content of what is produced.

I observed my first channeling "meeting" when I was ten years old...at my grandparents' house. My mom had long been going to these "meetings." I didn't know what the meetings were about except that my parents disagreed about them. My father's side was devout Orthodox Christian. We went to church every Sunday, so the meetings' esoteric nature did not appeal to him.

The first time I attended a meeting, my mother did not give me any preamble or context about the meeting or what would happen when we got there. We walked into my grandparents' living room. About forty people were sitting in layered circles. My uncle, my mother's brother, was the focus of everyone's attention. He spoke in a very different way than I was used to; it was all in rhyme. It was obvious to me that the speaker was not actually my uncle. I stood in the back and listened. I felt excited but also scared.

I wondered, *Could whoever was speaking through my uncle speak through me? Could they just jump into me and take over my body? Could I be a channeler? Could they harm me or my uncle or grandmother? Was it all a big sham?* On another level, it felt completely natural. I felt a sense of truth to the process and a resonance with the content. I felt an inner, or *noetic*, knowing. "Noetic" comes from the Greek *noésis/noétikos* and means inner wisdom, direct knowing, intuition, or implicit understanding. I couldn't describe with words why I thought it was the truth; I just felt it. I couldn't imagine how my uncle could fake the different voices, the mannerisms, the accents, and especially the knowledge. He was only a high school graduate at the time, and some of the knowledge he shared in trance was far beyond his education. The same was true for my grandmother. My grandmother and uncle sometimes spoke languages they did not know while channeling. My relatives had no incentive to falsify channeling, and I believed they were not making it up.

At the weekly meetings, we would sit in a circle and wait for the channeled "being" to come through. I found it fascinating and frightening: the strangeness of it all. Sometimes there were specific messages for me. I do not remember the messages today, but I remember it as a time of great significance in my life. For example, when I was sixteen years old, I had a horseback riding accident and was in excruciating pain to the point where I could not walk. My uncle went into a channeling state and worked on my back. His hands were so hot! I felt the heat and energy moving through my body. After what felt like a very long session but was probably about thirty minutes, my back was not in pain anymore, and I could walk easily. The "meetings" imprinted on me that there were invisible realms that my normal senses could not perceive. These were concepts not taught in school, church, or anywhere else that I had exposure to.

My grandfather considered it his life's work to unravel our spiritual selves and examine what happens to us after we die. He wrote a book called *Life After Death* based on his research and understandings. Growing up in this atmosphere, I learned that my family members believed several things about trance channeling.

1. Their trance channeling was consensual. They could say no or stop it at any time.

2. They set intentions for only positive high-level "beings" to come through the channeler.

3. They were guarded by spirit guides. The guides were gatekeepers and directed which "beings" came in. This spirit-guide team's sole purpose was to guide their assigned human to wake them up to their true self and the path of their higher self's choosing.

4. Envisioning themselves surrounded by white light and pure loving intentions acts as protection. This ensures that no malevolent energy or "beings" can harm them. This came with the assumption that some "beings" were of "lower" vibrations who did not have positive intentions that potentially could hurt them.

After many years, the meetings stopped. My mother and I continued to have regular channeling sessions together. Through that process, various deceased family members communicated through her and told me things that she could not possibly know. One time after both my grandparents had passed, my grandmother channeled through my mother. When she was alive and yet close to death, I had a private conversation with her. She shared her fear of dying with me. She loved being married to my grandfather in life. Still, she was not excited about being married to him for eternity. She believed that she would be based on her religious upbringing. I was empathetic to her concerns and tried to comfort her as best I could. I did not share this conversation with anyone. Shortly after she had passed, she communicated through my mother. She said to me confidingly, "You know I was worried about nothing. We aren't married on this side. We see each other from time to time, but he is doing his things, and I am doing mine." She was so relieved and happy.

Some might argue that my mother psychically picked up this piece of information from my own mind and "channeled" it back to me. Perhaps. And perhaps my grandmother's consciousness survived her physical death, and she was communicating to me. At this point, we are still trying to figure out if and how we can test these two distinctions. Regardless, it is still quite remarkable that my mother channeled what my grandmother shared with me in confidence.

Developing and Applying My Channeling Ability

My own personal experience of channeling ebbed and flowed through my life. I was always a very sensitive child. I could feel others' emotions. I felt sad when others were sad and had a tough time being in crowds. I was also terrified of the dark as I thought there were other things around me that I could not "see," but I could sense that they were there. I always wanted a light on.

Growing up in California as the New Age movement blossomed, I became enthralled with learning about crystals, aura reading, and psychic powers. I was fascinated with the idea that I could have more than five senses and receive information beyond them. I practiced mentally connecting with my guides. I would ask for guidance on many decisions—from the mundane, like which party to go to Friday night, to the more life-altering, like which college I should attend. The advice usually made sense and supported me. I wasn't exactly sure what the source of information was, but I felt a noetic sense of trust in the information I received. This sense was strengthened because the information consistently supported me and turned out to be true.

While I was not a trance channeler like my mother, grandmother, or uncle, I had extended human capacities that I considered channeling. I would most often get full-body chills when I heard or received information that reso-nated as truth. I could *feel* the present, past, or future physical and emotional states of others without using my five senses. For example, a friend shared about an imminent decision she needed to make. I got goosebumps all over my body when she spoke about choosing one option versus the other. I told her to go with that option. She did and was rewarded with joy, peace, and ease in her life. I repeatedly experienced this in a variety of settings.

I could also connect with my guides mentally. I would sit quietly in meditation. Once my mind was still and quiet, I asked them for support. I first began this process by asking yes-no questions and internally hearing a yes or a no. I was then able to ask more complex questions and hear more complex answers. Were these voices in my head just an aspect of myself rather than another "being" communicating with me? Perhaps, although it did not matter from my perspective because the guidance was always loving and nurturing, and it guided me to a more positive path in my life.

I also experienced an inner knowing about a place, a person, an event, an occurrence, or information that I could not possibly have known. This most often occurred when I was with patients in my private naturopathic practice. Of course, I completed a full medical history and review of symptoms. However, I also received a "download" about a current or past-life situation related to their current health condition. I asked them about it. They would almost always have some emotional response or release and acknowledge suppressed emotions about the situation. Their health would invariably improve with counseling to release the emotion.

Similarly, I "saw" things in their bodies, likely not their physical body per se but an energetic overlay around their body. These black spots or blocks revealed areas of their biological system that needed support or healing. Their health improved when I addressed the imbalances with various clinical tools. I rarely shared that I was supplementing my clinical skills with channeling skills. I felt uncomfortable sharing about it at the time. But the results were undeniable, so I continued to channel in my personal and professional life.

Numerous tools helped me strengthen my ability to listen to the information and energy that I felt was available to me through channeling. One was the use of applied kinesiology. I asked a question internally and then tested my index and middle fingers' strength when they were connected in a loop. A yes was signified by a firm hold. A no was indicated by the connection between the two fingers being broken. This applied kinesiology method allows me to tap into a more in-depth knowledge of my body.[2]

Meditation was also a powerful tool supporting my channeling. Being able to clear and focus the mind creates a mental silence that allows guidance to be noted more easily. It allows for deep listening to more than what our ordinary daily functioning mind can perceive. Rich and ancient shamanic traditions and journeywork also supported me, as did experimenting with various methods to purify my system, including fasting. Most important to my channeling development was the process of clearing personal egoic patterns by using the tools of CoreLight (http://www.corelight.org). Using processing techniques, I removed obstacles blocking my clear reception of information. You will learn ways to support your own channeling in chapter 10.

Coming Out of the Channeling Closet

After a few years in private naturopathic practice, I joined the research world in an academic university to study mindfulness meditation, its effects, and how it works. At that time, meditation research was barely getting any notice. Incorporating any meditation techniques into a clinical academic setting and obtaining funding for meditation research was a struggle. It took me years to convince my department to give me permission to teach a Mindfulness-Based Stress Reduction course at the hospital.

Amazingly, the National Institutes of Health funded my grant proposal to study mindfulness meditation for combat veterans with post-traumatic stress disorder. When I interviewed the veterans about their trauma, I noticed that much of the veterans' distress was emotional and even spiritual in nature. I also "saw" spirits surrounding them that were connected to the trauma and violence they were recounting. Most were trying, without success, to give the veterans a message of forgiveness and letting go. Of course, I could not talk about these perceptions at our lab meetings or include them in the study results. That was just not done.

The esoteric and spiritual aspects of meditation were (and still are) taboo in most academic settings. Nevertheless, my personal experience led me to believe that (1) our consciousness can extend beyond our physical bodies, and (2) there are vast, invisible realms on other dimensions that most humans don't easily access. However, I could not prove these beliefs in any way beyond my direct personal experience of them. I dreamed of running studies to test what I was personally experiencing. Alas, it was just not possible in an

In this book, I'll share the research on these questions so you can learn more about how your consciousness transcends your physical body, or its nonlocal nature. In chapter 1, you'll learn a brief history of channeling. You will also learn the many terms and definitions used for channeling. In chapter 2, you will see how channeling and mental health intersect and the evidence that indicates that most people who channel do not have a mental health disorder. In chapter 3, you will see how common channeling actually is. In chapter 4, you'll gain insight into the many studies showing that channeling is "real." In chapter 5, you will learn about how channeling might work. In chapter 6, you will see what channelers have in common and what makes them unique. In chapter 7, you will see channeling's proposed sources. In chapter 8, you'll be introduced to the Noetic Signature, a new model of first-person experiences, and how you can determine your own Noetic Signature. In chapter 9, you will learn about the usefulness of channeled content and how you can use it in your day-to-day life. Finally, in chapter 10, I'll share some practices so you can learn and develop your channeling and integrate it into your daily life for personal and collective good.

Because you picked up this book, I imagine you may have had your own channeling experiences, perhaps as a child, or maybe you have them now. Perhaps you don't have many people, or even anyone, whom you feel comfortable sharing these experiences with. You may be influenced by taboos; for example, someone made an offhanded negative comment about a medium TV show or the ridiculousness of a movie about channeling. You might have felt uncomfortable, worried, or shameful that they might direct similar comments at you. I wrote this book for you. You are not alone.

An Invitation to Be Curious

Biases and taboos about channeling are strong. The fact that you are reading this book leads me to believe that they have loosened their hold over you. We will continue to explore biases and taboos in various parts of the book. Despite your openness, you may find that some material may trigger your own biases, conscious or unconscious. I invite you to be mindful of this potential and bring an open, curious attitude to your learning process. If you find your body contracting and your mind becoming judgmental, allow yourself to pause.

Notice what triggered you and take stock of your own internal process at the moment.

Related to this, I'd like to make a note about some word choices. Sentences can get very clunky when they always include "supposed," "purported," "claimed," "ostensible," or other cautious words. These are meant to make sure you understand I am not saying these experiences or sources are definitively proven. I will not always use these words. They should be assumed when they are not there. I trust that you will form your own opinions about the validity of channeling and channeling sources regardless of the cautious words I use or don't use.

Throughout the book, pause and take some deep breaths. Invite all parts of you to be present to take in the information with more than just your cognitive or mental capacity. Experiment with reading with your whole being, tuning in to whether you resonate with the material. I am not here to convince you that channeling is real. I am here to offer you the knowledge and opportunity to be your own explorer of what is right for you. Enjoy!

The classic *Star Wars* series spans over forty years, holds a Guinness World Records title for the most successful film merchandising franchise, and made over $10 billion in box office sales worldwide. The Force is "an energy field created by all living things. It surrounds us, penetrates us, and binds the galaxy together." This is how Jedi teacher Obi-Wan Kenobi explained it to Luke Skywalker in *A New Hope*. Jedis move objects with their minds (psychokinesis) and hear their master's voices in their minds (telepathy). They are essentially "channeling" the Force.

There is no end to superhero movies where characters have various channeling powers. Doctor Strange (Marvel Comics) is a great example. Doctor Strange can project his spirit somewhere else (astral projection). He can control fire (pyrokinesis). He can also heal, hypnotize people, exert mental control over matter (psychokinesis), and teleport his physical body.

Numerous TV shows also feature channeling. In *Ghost Whisperer* (CBS), Melinda Gordon can see and communicate with spirits who have died. Each week's plot revolves around Melinda connecting with a spirit. She helps them resolve unresolved issues so they can move on from being stuck on Earth. The TV show list goes on and on: *Medium* (NBC), *Supernatural* (WB), *Psychic Detectives* (Court TV), *Ghost Hunters* (Syfy/A&E), *Knock Knock Ghost* (OUTtv), *Ancient Aliens* (History), *Ghost Adventures*, *Ghost Brothers*, *Ghost Nation*, *Kindred Spirits*, *Mountain Monsters*, and *Paranormal Caught on Camera* (Travel Channel).

Obviously, modern-day media is fascinated by channeling. I believe this excitement has likely made recent conversations about channeling experiences a bit easier. When people can set their experience in the context of a show or movie someone has seen, it is more relatable. It also normalizes channeling. Because people are seeing it everywhere, it becomes more normal. Rather than hiding channeling, they are revealing it and open to exploration (even if through fictional movies). The topic becomes more familiar, and people can be less hesitant to discuss their experiences.

Take a few minutes of quiet time to reflect and journal on the following questions:

Have you experienced taboos around channeling in your own life? If so, how did that affect you? Have you felt supported in your channeling experiences? If so, how was that experience? How does learning about the history of taboos about channeling help inform your experiences with taboos? Have you shared your channeling experiences with others? If so, how did that go for you?

Confusing Terminology

Today in most Western cultures, you can more safely talk about channeling experiences than two hundred years ago. However, the language we use to talk about channeling can be confusing. You may have noticed the many, many words used to describe channeling in your own exploration. My family used the words "channeling," "channel," and "automatic writing" for what my grandmother, mother, and uncle did. I didn't really question these terms when they used them. As I grew up in California as the New Age movement was flourishing, I heard many more words like "psychic," "medium," "clairvoyant," and so forth.

At IONS, I was immersed in a new field of study I hadn't known about before—parapsychology. Parapsychology is a branch of psychology that focuses on the scientific study of "psi" phenomena (Bem and Honorton 1994; Cardeña et al. 2015). Psi includes things like:

- telepathy—mind-to-mind communication;

- clairvoyance—information received about distant events, locations, or objects;

- psychokinesis—the mental influence of physical matter;

- precognition—information received from future events and retrocognition for information about past events; and

- survival—the possibility of the survival of consciousness after our body dies.

Parapsychology opened up a whole new world for me about channeling terms. I became confused by all the words and their definitions. The same words had different meanings depending on the paper I read or the person I talked to. What I called channeling, others called mediumship. What I heard as trance channeling, others called spirit possession. What some people called mental mediumship, others called clairaudience. It seemed like I was swimming in a tangle of terms and definitions. I even found a whole book filled with definitions, *A Glossary of Terms Used in Parapsychology*. The book has about 130 pages of terms! In the preface, the author noted, "[You] may have as much difficulty in reading the literature of the subject as if it were written in a foreign language" (Thalbourne 2003, xiii).

It did feel like a foreign language to me. I wanted to understand that language. As a naïve new researcher to the field, I formally reviewed the literature to understand the terms used for trance channeling (Miller and Wahbeh 2018). There were *twenty-nine different terms* used to describe the people who do this and the process!

I am not the first person to bring attention to the different terms and definitions and how they create confusion. An entire Parapsychological Association bulletin was dedicated to exploring this same issue (Evard and Ventola 2018). Researchers have debated these ideas as well (Tremmel 2014, 2015; Evard 2015). For example, some researchers think using the term "extrasensory perception" means we perceive beyond our usual five senses when we channel. This is an assumption. So, they developed other words like "anomalous cognition," "anomalous perturbation," and "anomalous force" (May et al. 1995). One researcher felt all the terms were limiting and created a new broader term, "exceptional human experiences" (White 1994).[3] Whether or not the scientific community will ever agree on terms and definitions for key terms is unknown.

What is your experience of terms used for channeling? Have you experienced confusion over the various terms? How has that influenced your relationship with your own experiences? Does having the right word or definition for what you are experiencing affect your experience of it or the meaning you ascribe to it?

So, where does that leave you? Contemplating these terms and their definitions can make your head hurt. Do you call these experiences psi or paranormal or parapsychology or psychic or anomalous or exceptional or channeling or mediumship or intuition or what? I propose that we focus on your experience of channeling rather than the terms. How do you experience channeling from your point of view? Are channeling experiences meaningful to you? Do you find them useful? How do they influence your daily life? How do they affect our collective human experience? We will continue to explore these questions throughout this book. Before we do, let me explain why I chose the term channeling and define it more clearly.

Clarifying Terms to Describe Your Experiences

When I first started working on this book, I was concerned about using the word channeling because of the taboo. Also, channeling had varied definitions already. I wondered if it was time to create a new word. And yet, wasn't making a new word just adding to the growing list used to describe these phenomena? I decided to stick with the term channeling and give you some context for how I use it.

Many have defined channeling with various nuances relating to where the information comes from, the "message," the audience, the purpose, and the range of experiences (Roxburgh and Roe 2011; Hastings 1991, 4). In a comprehensive review, John Klimo (1998) defines channeling as "the communication of information to or through a physically embodied human being from a source that is said to exist on some other level or dimension of reality than the physical as we know it, and that is not from the normal mind (or self) of the channel" (2).

Klimo's definition offers a good start. We can take this definition and build on it. For example, many people experience what they call "energy" that moves through them or can be shared with others. Let's add "information *and* energy" to the definition.

Klimo's definition also assumes that the channeler, or "embodied human being," is separate from the source. My personal experience and understanding lead me to believe that we are not separate from the source we reveal through channeling. At least not in the broader sense of what we usually mean by separate.

At IONS, our guiding hypothesis is that everything is interconnected. That we are, in essence, all one. This concept is the foundation of numerous spiritual traditions. Growing scientific evidence in cosmology (Currivan 2017) and quantum physics and the theory of quantum entanglement (Buniy and Hsu 2012) are also showing us that this is likely true. (You'll learn more about these ideas in chapter 5.) So, I didn't want to include any reference to the channeler being separate from the source.

Considering all this, here is the working definition for channeling that I mean when I use this term throughout the rest of this book.

Channeling is the process of revealing information and energy not limited by our conventional notions of space and time that can appear receptive or expressive.

Your Experience of Channeling

As you'll notice, this definition is incredibly broad. I call it an umbrella definition because it holds all the other experiences (and terms) you may have seen. For example, one common channeling type is clairvoyance. Clairvoyance comes from the French *clair*, meaning clear, and *voyance*, meaning seeing or vision. People who experience clairvoyance can see things in their mind's eye about an object, person, or place that they could not possibly know through their traditional senses. An example of clairvoyance is remote viewing. Remote viewers can describe distant locations without having been there. Other examples of clairvoyance include:

- aura reading—the perception of energy fields surrounding people, places, and things;

- geomancy—the perception of the energy of places and of the land;

- nature empathy—the perception of information and communication with nature and plants; and

- animal communication—the perception of information and communication with animals.

Many other terms attempt to describe our experience of channeling.

As you can see, channeling shows up in so many different ways. I think the various terms we've created for channeling are our attempts to define these experiences as best we can with our limited language. Perhaps the difficulty in choosing words to define channeling lies in the fact that channeling experiences are often ineffable or too extraordinary or extreme to be expressed or described in words. Our current verbal language is not able to fully express the depth and complexity of channeling experiences. I am often challenged to come up with words to describe my channeling experiences. I've heard this from many other people as well. If this is true for you as well, you are not alone.

Intuition is another example of an indescribable channeling experience. Intuition is also called clairsentience. People have shared many stories with me about important information they received through channeling. They "just know" what they received is accurate. I could ask them, "But, how do you know?" They would say something like, "I just know." I might probe to ask how they came to know that information. They would say something like, "It just came to me. I just know that it is true." This type of knowledge makes no logical or rational sense. How can we just learn something we didn't know and know it as truth? Many of your channeling experiences likely have this indescribable, "just know" quality as well.

So how do you begin to more fully explore the complexity of channeling so you can use it in your life without the limitations of terms and definitions? You can start with the idea that we all have the capacity at some level to reveal information and energy not limited by conventional notions of time and space. And that how you reveal this information and energy is unique to you. What is your way of accessing information and energy? Do you feel gut hunches in your body? Do you get goosebumps and know something is true? Do you have dreams that give you information? Do you see images or symbols? Do you hear a loving voice offering guidance?

Channeling comes in so many forms. Your way of channeling is unique to you. Despite the history, taboos, and various terms and definitions, your firsthand channeling experience is essential. At IONS, we call your unique way of channeling your Noetic Signature. There is no right or wrong signature. All are beautiful and unique. Just as each snowflake is different yet equal in its exquisite beauty, each person's Noetic Signature has inherent value. Our noetic diversity can be collectively celebrated. (You will explore your Noetic Signature in chapter 8.)

As you continue to explore the science of channeling in this book, I invite you to bring awareness to your own firsthand experience of channeling.

What is channeling for you? What parts of the definition of "channeling" described here resonate with you? If there are details that don't, how would you change it?

You Are Not Alone

For more millennia than we can track, humans have channeled. Numerous cultures around the world include channeling experiences as part of their everyday experience of life. Taboos around channeling are relatively new in human history. Unfortunately, because of these taboos, channeling is often associated with a mental health disorder. Channeling experiences don't fit in our current world view of logic, of rationality, and that the physical world is all that there is. So if you have ever wondered if these things happen because you have a mental problem, read on to find out more.

CHAPTER 2

Is This a Gift or a Mental Health Issue?

Sometimes what looks like a channeling experience may be a mental illness symptom, yet it is often not. This chapter will teach you what we know about channeling and mental disorders and distinguish between the two.[4]

> *"I just want to know what happened to me. I did things and had things happen that aren't supposed to happen in real life. Can someone tell me why?"*

> *"Do you have any advice for someone who's never believed in anomalous experiences (I come from a big family of MDs), atypical cognition, or the similar, but who seems to manifest some of these anomalies? There have been a number of things that have happened to me or seem to happen around me that make no sense and that I'm having a hard time discounting after years of experience. I don't know what to believe or who to trust—but I do know I'm tired of ignoring the strange stuff that seems to be happening around me, and of how little I know or understand."*

Messages like these from people wondering what is going on with them when they have a channeling experience land in my inbox regularly. Perhaps you've felt the same in having something happen to you and being confused or even afraid something was wrong with you. Maybe you've experienced hearing a voice guiding you to make a choice that you otherwise may not have made, and the choice was the right one. Perhaps you saw a loved one after they died. Maybe you had a dream that came true.

Perhaps you didn't share your experience with others for fear of judgment. Or maybe you did, and the person looked at you with consternation or disbelief or even called you crazy. Or perhaps they said, "That is impossible. You must have been imagining it." They diminished your experience, and so you doubted yourself. Most people who have channeling experiences are afraid of being labeled psychologically abnormal or unhealthy if they talk about them (Rabeyron and Loose 2015). People who share openly about their channeling experiences can be shamed, humiliated, or accused of being charlatans or fakes or insane.

Outside Their World View

So why do some people call us "crazy" when we talk about channeling? Like we talked about in the last chapter, there are extreme taboos about the topic. Channeling also does not fit within our current understanding of how things work. Our dominant paradigm right now is materialism. Materialism holds that matter is the fundamental substance of nature and that all things arise from matter. Nonlocal, nonphysical channeling doesn't fit very well in this paradigm.

Because of this, some people won't believe something if they don't understand how it works or it does not fit within their world view. It is not the first time people have doubted ideas outside of the norm. Many people dismissed the Wright brothers' flying machine invention because they too thought it was impossible. Fred Kelly (2014), author of the Wright brothers authorized biography, explained why:

"One reason why nearly everyone in the United States was disinclined to swallow the reports about flying with a machine heavier than air was that important scientists had already explained in the public prints why the thing was impossible. When a man of the profound scientific wisdom of Simon Newcomb, for example, had demonstrated with unassailable logic why man couldn't fly, why should the public be fooled by silly stories about two obscure bicycle repairmen who hadn't even been to college? In an article in *The Independent*—October 22, 1903, less than two months before the Wrights flew—Professor Newcomb not only proved that trying to fly was nonsense, but went farther and showed that even if a man did fly, he wouldn't dare to stop."

Similarly, when someone cannot imagine how you can "see" something halfway across the world, they may dismiss you as foolish. Regardless, remote viewing has been repeatedly demonstrated as accurate (Bierman and Rabeyron 2013; Baptista, Derakhshani, and Tressoldi 2015; May and Marwaha 2018b). It has even helped find archaeological sites (Schwartz 2019; S. Schwartz, De Mattei, and Smith 2019; Schwartz 2005). A small world view can limit what people believe is possible. Sadly, they often miss opportunities to experience many vast and profound truths about human capacity and our world.

Channeling Experience as Diagnostic Criteria

Another reason people dismiss channeling experiences as "crazy" has a historical basis. For most of the nineteenth and twentieth centuries, channeling was seen as a symptom of severe mental disorders by mainstream Western scientists and mental health professionals (Moreira-Almeida, de Almeida, and Neto 2005). Many channeling experiences have been listed as medical diagnostic criteria for mental illness (American Psychiatric Association 2013). Two mental health categories are commonly connected to channeling experiences: *dissociative symptoms* and *psychoses*. Dissociative symptoms have to do with feeling disconnected from yourself. Psychoses have to do with mental disorders that cause abnormal thinking and perceptions.

Some Channeling Experiences Can Look Like Dissociative Symptoms

Almost half of American adults have had at least one dissociative episode in their lives (National Alliance on Mental Illness 2017). These numbers are increasing in the general population (Moreira-Almeida, Neto, and Greyson 2007). Dissociative symptoms can include:

- experiencing your behavior, thoughts, and feelings from a dreamlike distance;

- feeling detached from your environment and the objects and other people in it;

- being confused about a part or all of your identity; and/or

- a partial or total loss of memory (Lewis-Fernandez 1998; Holtgraves and Stockdale 1997; Mulder et al. 1998).

Like many other symptoms, dissociative states exist on a continuum (Kihlstrom 2005; Seligman and Kirmayer 2008; Spitzer et al. 2006). Many people experience dissociative symptoms, like daydreaming or hypnosis. You know when you are driving and arrive home, not remembering the details of how you got there? Most of us could probably say we've zoned out while driving, especially on the freeway. Or when you gaze out the window, and your mind drifts into the past? These are examples of normal dissociation. Any trancelike state is generally considered a dissociative symptom (Seligman 2005a; Seligman and Kirmayer 2008; Castillo 2003).

An example of abnormal dissociation is not knowing who you are anymore (Stolovy, Lev-Wiesel, and Witztum 2015). Abnormal dissociative symptoms are often associated with historic physical, emotional, and sexual abuse (Coons 1994; Ogawa et al. 1997; Stolovy, Lev-Wiesel, and Witztum 2015). People with other psychiatric disorders, including post-traumatic stress disorder (PTSD; Armour, Karstoft, and Richardson 2014), attention deficit disorder (Coons 1994), schizophrenia, and anxiety disorders (Seligman 2005a), can also have dissociative symptoms.

Five main symptoms make up a dissociative identity disorder (DID) diagnosis (American Psychiatric Association 2013). The first is that the person must have two or more distinct identities or personality states with a stable and unique view of the environment and themselves. Here's an example:

Your friend invited you to go see a famous trance channeler. You had never seen one before. The gathering is a small group of about ten people. The trance channeler is sitting at the front of the room. She is a petite person, about five feet tall. You hear her talking to her support staff with a gentle voice. She speaks in clear, unaccented English.

The session begins. The trance channeler starts breathing heavily like she is running a marathon. Her head moves back, and her arms spread out. Then her breathing slows, and she looks out at the crowd, her eyes wide open and shining. "Greetings!" she says in a booming male voice. The voice reverberates off the walls of the small room. The trance channeler stands up and moves around the room with arms wide open, sharing in the booming voice. The trance channeler seems to have grown in height! This is not the petite person you saw when you entered. When the message is complete, the trance channeler sits back down, begins breathing quickly, and slumps over.

The support staff offers her water, and she comes back to her usual self. She says another "being" wants to come through. She begins the rapid breathing again and goes into a trance. This time, her body becomes tiny and folded in on herself. When she speaks, the voice is hoarse and strangled. The voice says it doesn't know where it is—that it was having surgery. The voice asks, "Am I dead? How can that be? I was in surgery." The support staff interacts with the voice, saying, "Yes, your physical body has died. Look around to see if there is anyone there who can help you." The process continues until the "being" leaves. The trance channeler appears to be her usual self again. She shares her experience of trance channeling and takes questions from the audience. You are amazed. You can't believe that the two "beings" were the same as this soft-spoken trance channeler.

This is one representation of what a trance channeling session could look like. The mannerisms, voice, and entire demeanor of a trance channeler change when they channel. From this description, the first criterion of DID is present. So, when someone sees a trance channeler and observes them "transforming" into another personality, they could appear to be expressing the mental illness of DID.

The second criterion for DID is memory gaps for everyday events. The third criterion is that the person must be distressed by their symptoms and have difficulty functioning in one or more of their major life areas. The fourth criterion is that the dissociative symptoms must not be part of regular cultural or religious practices. It is encouraging that the diagnostic standards allow for diverse cultural contexts. Spiritualist and shamanistic rituals that include trance channeling or spirit possession are included in this category. The last criterion is that the dissociative symptoms must not be due to some physiological effect of a substance (e.g., alcohol) or a medical condition (e.g., seizures).

In summary, dissociative symptoms, like daydreaming, are usual and commonly experienced. Some channeling experiences, such as trance channeling, can look like dissociative identity disorder while they are happening. Dissociative symptoms related to a mental illness are feeling disconnected from yourself, gaps in your memory, feeling distressed by your symptoms, and the symptoms occurring outside of a ritual-like channeling.

Reflect on your own experience with the spectrum of dissociative symptoms. Remember a time when you were daydreaming or zoned-out while driving. How did that trancelike experience relate to our human understanding of consciousness? Have you ever witnessed trance channeling? Write about the channeler's demeanor when in and out of the channeling state.

Some Channeling Experiences Can Look Like Psychotic Symptoms

Psychosis, a significant feature of schizophrenia, is another mental illness often ascribed to channeling. Schizophrenia is a severe and chronic mental disorder characterized by disturbances in thought, perception, and behavior. Delusions, hallucinations, disorganized speech, disturbed emotions, sleep, memory, language, and dissociation are symptoms of schizophrenia (American Psychiatric Association 2013).

Psychotic symptoms can also be present in healthy people. The World Health Organization did an extensive study of over two hundred and fifty thousand people in fifty-two countries worldwide. Up to 31 percent of healthy people had at least one psychotic symptom (Nuevo et al. 2012). Hearing voices or seeing things that others can't see doesn't necessarily mean that you have a mental illness in the context of channeling. These experiences are common, and people without mental illness can have them (Dein 2012).

When clinicians and researchers want to screen for psychosis symptoms, they often give screening questionnaires, like the "Community Assessment of Psychic Experiences—Positive Scale" (Capra et al. 2015). In this scale, there are three symptom categories. The first is the feeling as if someone or something is out to get you. The mentally healthy person with channeling experiences rarely has these thoughts. These symptoms can help distinguish between psychosis and channeling.

2007; Claridge 1997; Richards 1991; Rabeyron and Watt 2010), and that no relationship was found between channeling and mental health disorders in other studies (Dein 2012; Goulding 2004, 2005).

But why are studies showing that channelers have higher mental health symptoms even if they don't reach clinical levels? It is because the screening tests ask questions about symptoms that look very similar to channeling experiences. For example, in one of our studies, these items had the highest scores: (1) the feeling that other people, objects, and the world around them were not real, and (2) hearing voices inside their head that tell them to do things or comment on things that they are doing. Hearing voices is very similar to the extrasensory perception of sound (clairaudience). If a clairaudient person completed the screening, they would likely score high on that item (even though they didn't have any of the other symptoms).

Some study participants did have clinical levels of dissociative symptoms. In one survey, people rated how intense their channeling experiences were, how often they happened, and how accurate the received information was. We combined all these ratings into one score. In the next example, you'll see how someone with channeling experience could score high on this combined score.

Miguel was always able to see spirits. As a child, he would see them clearly all around him. They wouldn't bother him, and he just ignored them and continued playing. Sometimes he would interact with them, but they usually went about their business, and he went about his. As he grew older, the spirits faded to the periphery of his vision as he became more engaged with his education and career. He could see them out of the corner of his eye, like a fast-moving white light. They didn't bother him, so he didn't bother them. He shared his experiences with some people, and they found it interesting. He felt it was a regular part of his life and didn't concern himself with it too much. One day, after a very intense and stressful period in his life, the spirits weren't in his periphery anymore. They were in his face and were interacting with him. He would see them when he woke up, throughout the day, and into the night. He would wake up from his sleep in a panic with spirits all around him. He wasn't sure what shifted to make them so engaged with him in a different way. He was

*afraid. He tried to continue with his work and family life but was very
disturbed and distracted.*

Miguel would have had a high score. In our survey, people like Miguel,
who had intense and frequent channeling experiences, had dissociation and
psychotic symptoms that reached clinical levels. This means that if you had
channeling experiences all the time and they were very intense, it could
prevent you, like it did Miguel, from living your normal life. A mental health
professional would likely be concerned with his score and connect with him
about his symptoms. Cases like Miguel's are rare. You will learn what Miguel
did to get help in the next section.

The more common scenario is that channeling experiences do not qualify
as mental disorders. The results of multiple studies worldwide are overwhelmingly clear. People who channel may have more symptoms than people who do
not. However, their symptoms levels are not high enough to be positive on
mental illness screening tests.

Most Channelers Remember Their Experiences

When my grandmother would trance channel, she wouldn't remember
any of it. She described it as going to sleep and waking up again. Other trance
channelers I've worked with share that they observe the experience and do
remember it.

Our team measured people's level of awareness when channeling. First,
we asked trance channelers to rate their awareness level on a scale from 0 to
100. Zero represented being fully conscious and aware, and 100 meant being
fully unconscious and not aware. The average for our two trance channeler
groups was forty-seven (Wahbeh et al. 2019; Wahbeh and Butzer 2020). Other
researchers found similar results (Negro, Palladino-Negro, and Louzã 2002).

These results are quite interesting for a couple reasons. The first and most
relevant to this chapter is that most trance channelers do not meet DID's
amnesia criteria. Today, most trance channelers do not go entirely into a
trance, are aware of their experience during the trance, and remember the
experience afterward. They describe the experience as stepping aside and
observing what is happening.

The second reason is that trance channelers have "trance" in their name because they are assumed to be in a full trance and not conscious of what is happening. Some indigenous cultures have channeling rituals where this is true. However, few channelers have no memory of their channeling states today in the Western world. Two examples are Carla Rueckert, who channeled the Law of One material, and Eva Pierrakos, who channeled the Pathwork series. The memory loss criterion is not commonly experienced in the West.

We also asked people with other channeling types, such as telepathy or precognition, about their level of awareness. Their ratings showed a higher level of awareness at thirty-four (Sagher, Butzer, and Wahbeh 2019). The memory gap criterion doesn't apply here either.

What does the role of memory play in your channeling? Do you remember the information you receive from channeling after the experience is complete? Some people are aware during their channeling experience, but then don't remember the details a few days later. What are your experiences with memory and channeled material?

Most Channelers Are High Functioning and Well Adjusted

Probably more important than the screening tests and memory loss is the evidence that people who channel are high functioning and well adjusted. Both the DID and psychosis criteria include the requirement that the person cannot function in their daily life because of their symptoms (American Psychiatric Association 2013). This means that they have trouble managing things in their everyday life, like cleaning, dressing, cooking, working, or caring for children or their families. Being poorly adjusted also means that the person has trouble connecting with and maintaining relationships with other people.

This is rarely the case with people who channel. Most people who have various types of channeling experiences are well-adjusted, high-functioning individuals. Multiple studies worldwide have repeatedly shown these results on psychological well-being and distress, overall mental health, and social adjustment assessments (Negro, Palladino-Negro, and Louzã 2002; Moreira-Almeida and Cardeña 2011; Moreira-Almeida, Neto, and Cardeña 2008; Roxburgh and Roe 2011; Stolovy, Lev-Wiesel, and Witztum 2015; Moreira-Almeida, Neto, and Greyson 2007; Moreira-Almeida and Koss-Chioino 2009).

Interestingly, the mediums who experience being fully possessed by another entity had better social adjustment scores and *fewer* psychiatric symptoms (Moreira-Almeida and Cardeña 2011). Trance channeling is generally a more intense channeling type that most closely resembles DID's first criterion (dissociative symptoms). And so, it is revealing that the trance channelers are well adjusted with fewer psychiatric symptoms.

Channeling Supports Positive Well-Being

Perhaps the most significant distinguishing factor between channeling experiences and mental illness is that the symptoms must negatively affect you. This is not usually the case with channeling experiences. People say that their various channeling experiences are actually beneficial, inspirational, and positively impact their lives (Griffiths et al. 2008; Kennedy and Kanthamani 1995a; Ellison and Fan 2008; Wahbeh, Radin, et al. 2018; Richards 1991). Trance channeling and mediumship positively impact the channeler's life (Negro, Palladino-Negro, and Louzã 2002; Moreira-Almeida and Cardeña 2011; Wahbeh, Carpenter, and Radin 2018; Wahbeh et al. 2019; Wahbeh and Butzer 2020).

People reported that their psychic or transcendent experiences were valuable in one study. Very few rated the psychic experiences as harmful (Kennedy and Kanthamani 1995b). People's belief in life after death and a guiding or protective higher force increased after their experiences. So did their interest in spirituality, sense of connection to others, happiness, well-being, confidence, optimism about the future, and meaning in life. Their fear of death, depression or anxiety, isolation and loneliness, and worries and fears about the future decreased. This study highlights that channeling experiences can be positively impactful, meaningful, and integrative.

The channeler also often feels their skills help their communities. Mediums think their healing skills and the information provided to their clients are valuable and serve a therapeutic function for them and their clients

(Moreira-Almeida and Cardeña 2011; Roxburgh and Roe 2011; Emmons and Emmons 2003). Being a medium provides practical gains including increased community status, power and respect, and even livelihood in many cultures. Mediumship also allows people to reframe their life experiences. For example, a person who endured hardship or illness in their early life could view those as preparation for a medium or healer role (Seligman 2005a).

Clearly, channeling imparts a positive impact. But what determines how positively impactful channeling is from one person to the next? We explored if there are any characteristics that determined who received more or less benefit from channeling. Three aspects predicted a more significant positive impact: lower psychotic symptoms, older age, and higher sensitivity. Higher levels of psychotic symptoms would likely decrease the quality of life in general and the positive impact of channeling. Perhaps being older allows greater maturity to cope with any stress and integrate the beneficial aspects into their lives with ease. For highly sensitive people, perhaps channeling provides grounding and centering to their lives. I know that when I channel, I feel more relaxed and calm. After channeling, I feel clear-headed, emotionally calm, and a sense of fulfillment, as if I've just had a long meditation session.

How has channeling impacted your life? Describe any positive and negative aspects of your channeling experiences.

So let's review the significant differences between channeling and a mental illness.

1. Dissociation and psychotic symptoms are usually higher in people who channel than those who don't, but not high enough to cause concern about their mental health. Experiencing some dissociative and psychotic symptoms is common in people with normal mental health worldwide.

2. Most people who channel do not experience memory gaps in everyday life.

3. Most people who channel are high functioning and well adjusted with no unwanted disruption of their daily activities.

4. Most people are positively impacted by channeling.

Having channeling experiences does not necessarily mean that you have a mental illness. You have now learned some ways to tell the difference between the two. However, you may feel that perhaps your channeling experiences could be part of a mental illness. Read on to learn how to assess your own experiences.

Ways to Assess Your Mental Health

One of the most important ways to tell if your channeling experiences are part of a mental illness is by looking at their impact on your life. Whether you rate the impact as positive or negative can help you decide whether your channeling experiences are healthy or not so healthy (Lukoff 2010; Vieten et al. 2018). For example, if your channeling experiences bring meaning to your life and improve your well-being, they are likely not part of a mental illness. Channeling experiences usually (but not always) happen at the right time and place, as part of a ritual or with a specific intention.

Rarely do people report negative aspects to their channeling, but it does happen. Like Miguel, some people have disturbing or intrusive channeling experiences. Your channeling experiences should not cause you distress, anxiety, worry, or other negative emotions or consequences in your life. Your work or social relationships should not be negatively affected. Usually, channeling experiences are short and only happen occasionally. They do not happen all the time and disturb your everyday life. If any of these negative effects are true for you, please reach out for support. Many compassionate and skilled spiritual, religious, and channeling communities and mental health professionals exist to support you if you are struggling with your channeling experiences.

If you do reach out for support, please note a few things. Be aware of the perspective of the person you are reaching out to. Suppose you connect with a spiritual, religious, or channeling community. They may view your experience only as channeling and may dismiss any psychological or neurological aspects. Similarly, suppose you engage a mental health professional. They may ignore your experience's channeling elements and assume it is a mental illness (Moreira-Almeida and Cardeña 2011). Do not be disheartened if this happens to you.

You need to be aware of the possibility of misdiagnosis in both worlds to get the help you need. Thankfully, there is a trend in clinical and spiritual communities to acknowledge and honor both channeling and mental health. Rest assured, there is support for you. Continue your search until you find practitioners who offer compassionate, well-rounded guidance for you.

Miguel reached out to his friends and family. He didn't know what to do. Someone recommended that he go see a mental health professional. He visited them and received supportive therapy for what he was going through. He also talked to a local curandero (traditional native healer/ shaman) that a family member suggested. Miguel found a healing path that worked for him to manage his channeling experiences. With support, he was able to find a balance to honor his channeling and function well in his everyday life. Miguel was fortunate to have multiple avenues of healing and find a way that supported him the best.

Perhaps in time, channeling experiences will no longer be viewed with the mental illness lens. The stigma surrounding mental health conditions and channeling experiences will hopefully be improved. Regardless of whether this happens or not, one thing is obvious: channeling experiences are widespread around the world. Let's see just how common they are.

CHAPTER 3

How Common Are These Experiences?

Richard was the first in a long line to ask me a question after my lecture on the IONS Channeling Research Program. He moved in closer and whispered. Richard thanked me for the work we were doing. He then looked around to make sure no one else was listening and continued. Richard shared that he suddenly woke up from sleep one night and saw his mother standing at the foot of his bed. Richard was shocked but comforted that she looked peaceful and happy. He went back to sleep and forgot all about it. The next day his brother called saying that their mom had passed away and that she died at the same time Richard had seen her the night before. He didn't feel comfortable sharing his visitation with his brother or anyone else.

A few years later, he had a vivid dream of a friend. She told him to connect with her husband while she was gone. Later the next day, news of her death from a car accident arrived. Richard comforted the husband as best he could but never shared the dream. Richard was confused by his experiences. His rational mind couldn't make sense of them. As far as he knew, other people didn't have them. He couldn't believe they were just coincidences or synchronicities. He wanted reassurance that he was not alone.

Stories like Richard's are not unique. In fact, I hear similar ones after every talk and through regular emails from around the world. I've asked my fellow scientists if they hear the same stories. They do!

The stories have common themes. The first is that the experience is unexplainable. It doesn't fit with what you currently know about the world. You also have not shared it with anyone else. You feel like you need to hide it from others because of how others might view you. On a personal level, the experience awakens your curiosity about your experience and the nature of reality. You wish you don't have to be in the metaphorical closet about your experience. You want to share with others and compare notes. You want to feel a sense of connection and validation about your experience. I know I felt the same way about my channeling experiences.

Hearing these anecdotes time after time heightened my interest in understanding exactly how common these experiences are. Let's review what I discovered.

How Common Is the Belief in Channeling?

I began exploring research on people's beliefs. Many studies have polled people from around the world to see if they believe in various channeling experiences (Gallup and Newport 1991; Sheils and Berg 1977; Irwin 1993, 2009; MacDonald 1995; Otis and Alcock 1982; Roe 1998; Sjödin 1995; Wahbeh, Radin, et al. 2018; Orenstein 2002; D. Moore 2005; Haraldsson 1985, 2005, 2011; Wahbeh, Niebauer, et al. 2020). The numbers might be higher than you imagined.

In the United States, approximately 75 percent of Americans believe in at least one paranormal phenomenon (Rapoport, Leiby-Clark, and Czyzewicz 2017), like communicating with someone who has died. In another study, about one-quarter of polled adults in the United States believed that contact with the dead was possible (Gallup, Inc. 2005). People from North, Central, and South America, the United Kingdom, Nordic countries, Western and Eastern Europe, Africa, India, and the Far East have also been asked if they believe in life after death or contact with the dead. Many do believe (from 21–78 percent; Haraldsson 1985, 2005, 2011; Sigelman 1977). Over half of the people in another study believed that places could be haunted by spirits (Rapoport, Leiby-Clark, and Czyzewicz 2017).

These surveys have been repeated over the years, and interestingly, the number of people who believe increases each year (Rapoport, Leiby-Clark, and Czyzewicz 2017). Our belief in channeling or paranormal experiences is growing.

Are Belief and Experience Related?

Believing that something is possible is different from actually having the experience. I remember learning about out-of-body experiences (OBEs). I already believed that I had a spirit separate from my body. I never imagined that it could leave my body while I was still alive. A childhood friend told me they could leave their body while dozing off to sleep. They moved their spirit body around their house, neighborhood, and beyond. Their escapades were terrific, and I was jealous that I could not do the same. Their OBE adventures were the ultimate wish of any teenager because they could go "out" after curfew!

I believed OBEs were possible but had never experienced them. How did my belief in OBEs relate to my understanding of it? One night, I awoke suddenly. I felt my right arm in the air and the rest of my body lying on the bed. I opened my eyes and saw my physical right arm lying on the bed, but I could still "feel" my right arm in the air. I was very excited. I realized this could be an OBE. Having knowledge of OBEs beforehand created an opening for the possibility that it could happen to me.

Some survey studies measure belief and experience. The results allow us to learn about the relationship between them. Channeling beliefs and experiences have strong positive relationships. This means that the greater your belief, the greater your experience. This result is seen over and over again in many different groups, including the average person in the Western world (Wahbeh, Radin, et al. 2018; Wahbeh, Niebauer, et al. 2020; Wahbeh, Yount, et al. 2020), students and schoolchildren (Glicksohn 1990), college students (Spinelli, Reid, and Norvilitis 2002), and scientists, engineers, and channeling enthusiasts (Wahbeh, Radin, et al. 2018).

You can also learn about the relationship between belief and experience through laboratory studies. The forced-choice task is a typical laboratory task that measures our ability to access information in a nontraditional way.[6]

Imagine that you are sitting in front of a computer screen in a psychology lab. The screen has a large gray box in the middle. It also shows five symbols below the box: a red circle, a green square, a blue triangle, a purple octagon, and a yellow rectangle. Your job is to choose which of the five symbols is hidden behind the gray box. You click on the blue triangle. The screen goes blank, and then "It's a hit!" is displayed. Voilà, you chose correctly.

You make nineteen more guesses for a total of twenty "trials." If you get five or more correct, or 25 percent, then you performed better than chance on this task. Scoring better than chance means that your number of correct trials was better than if you just guessed at random. Because there are five symbols, if you guessed randomly, you would get about four trials correct. You guessed which symbol appeared in the gray box using some information humans don't usually have access to with our traditional five senses.

Researchers looked at over seven decades of forced-choice tasks and asked, "Are your beliefs related to how well you do?" They found that yes, the two are related. The greater your belief, the better you do on the task (Storm and Tressoldi 2017; Lawrence 1993).[7] Just like you saw in the survey results.

We know that the more we believe, the more likely we will have experiences. What we don't understand yet is which comes first. It is a classic chicken-and-egg scenario. Do we believe in channeling first and then have the experiences? Or do we have an experience first and then believe? Likely, it is a mix of both. I had channeling experiences as a very young girl and then understood that I believed in them as an adult. For OBEs, I believed first and then had the experience.

Did you have an experience first, or did you believe first? Reflect on your first channeling experience. Did you already have some beliefs about channeling or those types of experiences? How did having those beliefs influence your reaction to your experiences? How do your beliefs about channeling influence your experiences in general? Reflect on what your beliefs about channeling are. Notice if those beliefs support you to be more open or closed to your experiences or those of others.

Even though belief and experience are related, they are very different ideas. Believing in something does not necessarily mean that you have experienced it.

How Common Are Channeling Experiences?

When you are hiding your channeling in the closet, channeling seems very rare. You don't talk about it. Others don't talk about it. It appears as if channeling experiences aren't happening for people. You can even look at all the fun movies and TV shows and think, *These things are not real. They don't happen in real life.*

You can feel very isolated and alone with your experiences. I know I felt that way. All the other people who reach out to me do too. From this perspective, channeling seems like it would be a rare experience. I'd like to give you a broader perspective.

Numerous studies around the world show us just how common it is. Researchers have been formally studying how common channeling is for about forty years (Haraldsson 1985, 2011; Cohn 1994; Haraldsson and Houtkooper 1991; Castro, Burrows, and Wooffitt 2014a; McClenon 1993; Ross and Joshi 1992; Palmer 1979; Greeley 1987; Machado 2010; Bourguignon 1976; Hunter and Luke 2014, 101, 211, 231, 234, 237). The percentage of people in these studies who have had channeling experiences ranges from as low as 10 percent in Scottish citizens (Cohn 1994) to 97 percent in enthusiasts in the United States (Wahbeh, Radin, et al. 2018). These surveys ask about different types of channeling experiences, such as general psi experiences or extrasensory perception. Other studies ask about more specific experiences, such as telepathy, precognition, clairvoyance, contact with the dead, psi dreams, or OBEs. All the results say the same thing. Channeling is common.

Our team studied how common these experiences are with a bit of a twist (Wahbeh, Radin, et al. 2018). We asked three groups of people in the United States: average Americans, scientists and engineers, and channeling enthusiasts. Everyone was asked via email to complete a survey about unique human experiences. They checked whether they had had any of twenty-five different channeling experiences and, if so, how often they experienced it. Nearly nine hundred people finished the study. Including everyone, 96 percent reported having at least one of the twenty-five channeling experiences! As we had guessed, the channeling enthusiasts had the highest percentage, with the average American group and scientists and engineer group tied for second.

When the study results came back, our science team was quite surprised by how high the percentages were. We went back to the survey questions and asked ourselves if they could have been misunderstood somehow. For example, "feeling another's emotions" could be seen as a more traditional form of empathy rather than the channeling experience of clairempathy that we were trying to get at (Behling and Eckel 1991; Hodgkinson, Langan-Fox, and Sadler-Smith 2008; Sinclair and Ashkanasy 2005). We decided to take out these items and rerun the analysis. The percentages were above 80 percent, still surprisingly high.

The study results are overwhelming. Channeling experiences are not rare. In fact, they are common, very common!

Are Some Channeling Types More Common Than Others?

Samira has channeling experiences every day. She can feel her husband and children's emotional states all the time unless she consciously blocks them out. When her phone rings, she will often know who it is before seeing the caller ID. Occasionally, she will receive information from a dream that comes true in her life. This only happens a few times a year.

The fact that Samira has multiple types of channeling experiences and has them at different intervals is usual. This is true for me also. I "just know" things quite frequently but will trance channel infrequently. It is normal to have variations in how often you experience different channeling types.

Our studies' most endorsed channeling types were clairempathy (feeling other people's emotions) and claircognizance (just knowing something you wouldn't usually know through traditional means). Other common experiences were lucid dreaming, telepathy, information from dreams, and clairvoyance (extrasensory visual perception). Precognition (knowing the future) and contact with the dead were the next most common. Lowest on the list were geomancy (knowing information about the earth/land), psychic healing, manipulating fire, and levitation (Wahbeh, Radin, et al. 2018; Wahbeh, McDermott, and Sagher 2018; Wahbeh, Niebauer, et al. 2020).

Three questions about telepathy, clairvoyance, and contact with the dead have been asked in many studies worldwide. Combining results in over twenty thousand people worldwide, we get a powerful picture of how common channeling is![8] Telepathy was endorsed by 34–67 percent of the people, clairvoyance by 17–31 percent of the people, and contact with the dead by 25–53 percent by the people (Haraldsson and Houtkooper 1991; Greeley 1987, 1975; Pew Research Center 2009). These numbers are impressive for someone like me, who thought my strange family was the only one having these experiences. This means that nearly one in two people has experienced contact with the dead or telepathy. One in three people has had a clairvoyant experience. The results confirm that channeling experiences are common.

Let's put all the numbers in perspective. When medical journals talk about how common diseases are, they often refer to the percentage of people who have it. Sometimes they use the terms "very common," "common," "uncommon," "rare," and "very rare." The percentage of people who have to have a disease for it to be called *common* ranges from 0.003 to 11 percent. For a condition to be called *rare*, only 0.000004 to 0.02 percent of the people in a group need to have it (Snowman and Scheuerle 2009). The World Health Organization also has definitions for these terms. They define *very common* as greater than 10 percent, *common* as between 1 and 10 percent, *uncommon* as between 0.1 and 1 percent, *rare* as between 0.01 and 0.1 percent, and *very rare* as less than 0.01 perfect of a group having it.

The lowest values we saw for channeling experiences were for psychic healing at 8 percent (Wahbeh, Radin, et al. 2018). According to the World Health Organization and others, 8 percent is within the common range. These studies show that even the least-reported channeling experience is *common*.

Let's take another example. An incredible study measured how common mental disorders, including mood, anxiety, and substance use disorders, are in sixty-three countries. About 18 percent of the people had mood, anxiety, or substance-use disorder symptoms, showing that these symptoms are *very common* worldwide. Our values for telepathy, clairvoyance, and contact with the dead were at least in that range, if not higher.

These studies show us that not only are channeling experiences *common*, but they are *very common*! I hope this knowledge brings you comfort. Be confident that a lot of people have had a channeling experience in their lifetime, whether they believed it was real or not. If you have channeling experiences, you are not alone. In fact, you are in excellent company with people from around the world.

Does the commonness of channeling surprise to you? How does this information change your thoughts about your own channeling? How does it change your perceptions of your community and the likelihood that many members have had channeling experiences too?

Why Is Channeling Still Taboo?

If channeling is so common, then why do people like Richard hide their stories? We are long past the Middle Ages and other times when channeling was illegal. Why do I continue to get regular emails from people afraid to share their experiences with others? Why am I asked multiple times a week why people aren't talking openly about channeling?

Many of these communications are from academic scientists who would like nothing more than to research channeling. However, they don't because they are afraid to share their personal experiences or interests with their colleagues. Robert Ashby (1987) explained, "There is surely no field of study in which the concepts, beliefs, and biases of our 'common sense' world clash so violently with the data collected and analyzed by scholars as psychical research, or as it is frequently termed today, parapsychology." They are fearful of conducting research because they would likely lose their positions and/or be severely criticized. This is, unfortunately, a realistic outcome (Traxler et al. 2012).

In the last chapter, we saw that mental health disorders are common globally. True, there is some disapproval for saying that you have a mental health disorder. But people are not as afraid to talk about or research it. Over $5 billion was spent on mental health research in the United States in 2018. Only about $2 million was spent on formal parapsychology research at the same time. The amount of funding for all parapsychology research from 1882 to the present day is about the same as two months of psychology research in the United States (Schouten 1993). This lack of financial support is critical. It blocks us from learning more about channeling. It also reduces the number of people wanting to research it, even though they may be interested in doing so.

The lack of financial support also makes sense considering the extreme taboo against channeling in the research, education, and scholarship communities. The article "The Unbearable Fear of Psi: On Scientific Suppression in the 21st Century" (Cardeña 2015) gives many examples. Some include making claims about researchers that are not true, blocking the researcher's ability to publish in journals, and excluding and persecuting researchers looking into the topic.

The next section shares just two real-life examples. These examples are a far cry from the unfortunate witch-burning trials. But they are prominent examples of a different form of poor treatment.

If Only Pigs Could Fly...

Our team did a study asking meditators if they had any channeling experiences while meditating. We submitted the manuscripts to a highly rated journal for the peer-review process. The journal editor usually reviews the submitted papers to decide who will peer-review them. The journal editor sent us a very long explanation for why they refused to allow the peer-review of our article.

Apparently, our study should not have been done because channeling is impossible. Channeling experiences do not exist, so research on it wastes everyone's time and money. They said, "Is it worth spending (public) research money and resources, as well as the scientists' time necessary for peer review (let alone misleading the public's and the media's attention) to test the hypothesis that 1+1=3? Or the hypothesis that pigs can fly? Or that water can be turned into wine?... I will do everything in my power to avoid any public research grant money being spent in that direction."

Another paper we submitted on mediumship was initially accepted but was then removed. This time the rejection was because a study testing if mediums could learn information about deceased people was not scientific. These two examples speak for themselves regarding the deliberate unfairness and even personal passion against channeling research. Many opinions about channeling in the academic world are skeptical (Cardeña 2015; Sidky 2018).

The greatest tragedy in this blatant bias is that science does not tell us what we can and can't be curious about. Science is a process that can be used to answer *any* research question. These editors said that we are not allowed to ask certain research questions about channeling. Clearly, this is a taboo in action.

Considering the extreme bias in academia, you would think that scientists have never had channeling experiences. You learned about one of our surveys, where we specifically asked scientists and engineers about their channeling experiences (Wahbeh, Radin, et al. 2018). We were curious if the channeling taboo resulted from a lack of belief or direct channeling experience in scientists. We found no difference between the scientists and engineers group and other people on their overall channeling beliefs and experiences. We also found no differences between science categories. For example, a physicist did not answer differently than a health researcher.

Even with similar beliefs and experiences, taboos are still strong in academia, resulting in discriminatory and unethical practices to get the word out about channeling research. Funding for channeling research is low compared to other fields. This further prevents researchers from overcoming taboos and following their desires to study channeling.

Reflect on your own experiences with taboos. Why do you think people aren't talking about channeling? What do you think it will take for mainstream academia to be open to learning about and studying channeling?

Hope for the Future

In the face of these overwhelming odds against it, the reality is that interest in and research on channeling continues to grow. Some academics are taking a stand (Schooler, Baumgart, and Franklin 2018). A call was recently made for an open study of topics like channeling. The call was supported by over one hundred scientists from major universities worldwide (Cardeña 2014).

The research and education community may never fully accept channeling. That is okay because public interest in channeling is very high. We can learn so much by focusing on our personal experiences of channeling that we know are so common. There are also many cultures worldwide where channeling taboos do not exist, where channeling is an intrinsic part of their culture. The view I shared here is biased by my background in the United States.

The research on how common channeling is allows you to be reassured if you, like me, do not live in a culture where channeling is accepted, where you are faced with criticism and disbelief regularly. For you and me, this chapter brings hope that we are not alone.

It allows me to hear people like Richard with deep compassion in my heart when he whispers to me in his hushed tone, "Have you ever heard of anything like this before?"

I can lovingly smile and reply, "Yes, Richard, I have heard of this before. Please know that you are not alone. Many people around the world have had experiences similar to yours. Please know that what you experienced is not rare. In fact, it is common."

Let's bring channeling out of the metaphorical closet and have open conversations about channeling, how it affects our lives, and how it can support us.

CHAPTER 4

Is Channeled Material True?

I am at a neighborhood gathering celebrating our long summer nights. Our neighborhood has been attempting to build community, and this is our first gathering. Most of us don't know each other very well. I am talking to our neighbor Fernando, who lives down the road.

"So, what do you do?"

"I am a researcher and study extended human capacities."[9]

Fernando gets an interesting look on his face and says, "Hmmm, yeah, I've heard of those things, but I didn't think they were real. Aren't those just made up or fakes?"

He still seems curious, so I continue, "Actually, there is quite a bit of research about them. Even though we may not be able to explain exactly how they work, the experiences are common and real."

We've seen that channeling experiences are common. They are also real. What I mean by real is that we can observe them with objective methods. We can show that they exist beyond our imagination. An important paper on the realness of channeling was recently published in the *American Psychologist*. The *American Psychologist* is the official journal of the American Psychological Association (Cardeña 2018). The paper summarized meta-analyses on channeling experiences.

A meta-analysis combines data from multiple studies. In general, meta-analyses are the highest level of evidence or proof for a specific research question.[10] They are also the gold standard used in evidence-based medicine. The *American Psychologist* paper showed that there is evidence that many channeling experiences exist and can be observed. The channeling types included telepathy, precognition, presentiment, remote influence, distant healing, remote viewing, and psychokinesis. Let's review the evidence for these and other channeling types that shows they are real.

Your Consciousness Affects the Physical World

Of course, we affect the world around us. But do we affect the world around us with our minds? Can our intention, awareness, or consciousness influence the physical world? Many channeling terms describe this phenomenon: anomalous perturbation, anomalous influence, anomalous force, expressive psi, psychokinesis, and mind-matter interactions. All of these terms refer to some aspect of our consciousness affecting the physical world.

You've probably seen depictions of psychokinesis in movies: *Doctor Strange, Thor, The Avengers, Captain America*. All of these movies inspire you to *be* more fully. They are also full of scenes where superheroes use their mind to move things around. The typical scene has the superhero with their hand outstretched and intense concentration on their face. The superhero lifts the bad guy into the air and flings them aside. Numerous scientific studies show these mind-over-matter effects in the laboratory, the field, and beyond.

Intention Effects in the Laboratory

One of the most common terms used for mind over matter is psychokinesis. Macro-psychokinesis is the mind's influence on objects that we can see with our eyes—like the superhero flinging aside the car (Braude 2015). Micro-psychokinesis is the mind's influence on probabilistic systems that we can't necessarily see with our eyes. Probabilistic targets are things like dice rolls, coin flips, or shuffled cards. Micro-psychokinesis, or micro-PK, doesn't usually show up in movies. Micro-PK can only be seen with statistical analysis. Statistics are not as exciting for Hollywood.

Micro-PK was first suggested by Sir Francis Bacon in 1670. He thought we could evaluate the "force of imagination" on inanimate objects such as dice and the shuffling of playing cards (Bacon 1670). Fast forward three hundred years later to numerous dice studies done in the 1970s by J. B. Rhine. People would direct their mind or intention on a specific number coming up for a dice roll. Rhine and others found that our intention can influence what side a rolled die will land on (Radin and Ferrari 1991).

Dice rolls and coin tosses lost favor as probabilistic targets in the laboratory. They were replaced by radioactive isotopes that decay through a random process. At any moment, there could be particle decay or no particle decay. In these studies, participants tried to mentally slow down or speed up the rate of decay (Beloff and Evans 1961). You can imagine that dealing with radioisotopes in the laboratory was not ideal.

Electronic sources of randomness were then found to be the targets. These electronic sources generate a stream of random noise or of 0s and 1s. These little machines are called random number generators, or RNGs. According to what we know from physics, this data stream should always be random and not deviate. Why should directing our intention toward a random process change anything? If we believe that our mind is wholly confined to our brain, then it really shouldn't. Micro-PK studies test whether that is true or not.

From what we see so far, our intention can affect our physical world. Multiple laboratory studies have demonstrated that yes,[11] participants can influence these random processes (Schmidt 1974; Varvoglis and Bancel 2015; Jahn et al. 2007; Dunne and Jahn 1992; Bosch, Steinkamp, and Boller 2006; Radin et al. 2006).

Intention Effects in the Field

These are just lab experiments. What about in the real world? Can your intention possibly influence objects when you aren't intending to? That was the central research question of many studies done "in the field." In these studies, people did not know that the effects of their intentions were being measured.

Burning Man is a large event of over seventy thousand people that happens once a year. People come from all over the world to the middle Black Rock Desert of northwest Nevada, United States. On the last night of the festival, a massive structure of a man is burned. Everyone is focused on the "burning of the man." The excitement and intensity in the air are palpable. This is just one example of a potent event where large numbers of people gather with a shared intention of coherent focus. IONS collected RNG data during Burning Man festivals over multiple years. We saw that the RNG data is not so random during the intense periods like the "burning of the man." Results from field studies like this are important because the participants aren't directing their intention toward the RNGs like they do in laboratory studies. They don't even know that RNG data is being collected. And yet, the RNG data deviates from randomness during large shared-intention events (Nelson 1997; Nelson et al. 1996; Radin 2018).

The Global Consciousness Project (GCP) collected RNG data from around the world for over twenty years. Data from five hundred events was analyzed to see if events with high global focus would be different from other times. The five hundred events included large predictable events, like New Year's celebrations and sports events, and unpredictable events, like earthquakes and terrorist attacks. The RNG data was less random during all of these events (Nelson 2015)![12] This means that our unconscious intentions influenced RNGs. There is no reason for this within a materialistic paradigm where your consciousness is confined to your brain. There must be something else going on. Perhaps your consciousness and where you put your attention makes a difference in the material world.

Exciting results from the GCP study give us some insight into the nonlocal aspects of our consciousness too. One noteworthy result was that the data sets from distant RNGs were related. For example, let's take a momentous negative event like the 9/11 terrorist attack in New York City. The data changes from an RNG in Saudi Arabia were related to RNG data in California. This tells us that distance likely does not matter. If it did, the data from the RNG units closer to New York would be more affected, and thus, not related to data from ones farther away. Because the data from distant RNG units was related means that our intention's effect is not determined by space. Our consciousness can affect the physical world at a far greater distance from where we currently are. Have you ever been thinking about a friend or family member who lived far away from you? Maybe they actually felt you thinking of them. The GCP data gives us a glimpse of this using an objective method.

Another significant result was that high emotion events had larger effects than low emotion events. It didn't matter whether the events were positive, like a global meditation, or negative, like a terrorist attack. What was more important was the intensity of the emotion. This is an incredible finding. This means that it may not necessarily matter if you feel intense joy or intense anger. You would affect the RNG. Your feeling of joy and your feeling of anger probably seem very different to you but not to the RNG. A new version of the GCP will hopefully be able to learn more about this fascinating result.

While you likely aren't quite a superhero flinging bad guys and cars around, these results using different research protocols show that your intention influences the physical world.

Your Staring Makes a Difference

Lin was sitting at her favorite coffee shop, studying for her biology exam. It was crowded and noisy as it usually was before midterms. Lin was engrossed in her notes when she impulsively looked up and turned around to see someone staring right at her. It was the friend she was scheduled to meet later that day. Lin felt her friend staring at her as if the stare did something to Lin before she saw her friend.

Has something like this ever happened to you? The feeling of being stared at is a widespread experience. What makes you turn around? Some people don't have any sensations in their body but just look. Others feel a tingling sensation or heat just before they look to see if someone is there.

Many studies have been conducted on "the sense of being stared at." Researchers asked, "Does the act of staring affect another person in some way?" The studies work like this: The "looker" stares at a participant. The person being started at is in another room and doesn't know when the "looker" is staring. They can often tell when the "looker" is staring at them (Schmidt 2015),[13] even when the "looker" is staring through a closed-circuit TV. The "looker" does not even need to be near the person to get the effect! Dr. Sheldrake (2015), a principal researcher of remote staring, said, "The commonness of the sense of being stared at in everyday life, together with the positive results from numerous experiments, makes it very probable that this is a real ability."

Did your mother ever tell you to stop staring when you were a child? I know mine did. I also know I've said it to my own children more than once. As children, we are so curious. We want to look. Maybe there was some more profound truth to our mother's warnings. What if your staring did something to the person you were looking at? That the people we were staring at could tell! Taking it one step further, what if we could use that to help them in some way?

Another interesting laboratory experiment tested just that. Imagine studying for a big exam that makes you nervous, like a college entrance exam or certification test. Now imagine that someone is focusing their positive intention on you to increase your attention so you do well. Now imagine that doing this works! Several studies have shown that, yes, this is true. Again, the effects are small, but they are there.[14] I wish I knew about this in my college years. Who knows how much better I could have done on my exams! At least my stress level would have been lower, knowing I had someone helping me focus.

Intention Affecting Other People's Bodies

Researchers took this one step further by testing if people's bodies would be changed by the intention. This paradigm is called the direct mental interactions with living systems, or DMILS. Here's how DMILS works.

You are sitting in a comfortable chair in a ten-by-ten-foot two-thousand-pound electromagnetically shielded chamber. The chamber doesn't allow any electromagnetic signals to pass through its walls, like those from mobile phones, radios, or computers. You have on a head cap with small discs on it, collecting the electrical signals of your brain neurons (electroencephalography, or EEG). You also have stickers on your chest, collecting your heart signals. The small bands on your hands and fingers measure your skin signals, temperature, and blood pressure. You are the "receiver." The researcher finishes connecting the equipment and asks you to simply relax and be open.

Meanwhile, someone you love is in a separate room. They are the "sender." They have the same equipment attached to their body. What is different for them is that they have a TV in front of them. Occasionally, your picture appears on the TV. When they see your image, they send you as much positive intention as they can. When your picture goes away, they think about something else.

You don't know when your loved one is sending you positive intentions. You are just relaxing in a comfortable chair in a different room. Researchers then see how your body signals compare to each other during the sending and non-sending times.

Dozens of these types of experiments have been done using DMILS.[15] The results are clear. The receiver's body changes when the sender is sending versus not sending (Schmidt 2012, 2015; Achterberg et al. 2005; Richards et al. 2005; Schmidt et al. 2004).[16] The effect appears to be instantaneous. The results are small, observable,[17] and astonishing.

Reflect on experiences you've had where you felt someone else's stare or someone else felt yours. How did that affect your views about the nature of reality? Are there other ways you've felt your intentions influenced the physical world? If so, how did that change your perceptions of yourself? Reflect on what the world could be like if everyone understood that our intentions affect the physical world.

You saw with the GCP that our unconscious intentions can influence the physical world. You also learned that conscious staring or intention can also affect the physical world—namely, the friends and family you are sending your intention to. What is even more remarkable is that the effect is instantaneous. It is not as if there are thought-forms that leave your mind and travel to your loved one. You think of them, and they are instantly affected by your thoughts or intentions. The implications of this are staggering. What if you could actually see how your intentions affected the people around you in a more tangible way? You can see some glimpses of this from intention studies done in the health field.

Using Intention to Heal

Have you ever sent a healing prayer to someone who was ill? How about sending positive intentions to someone going through a difficult time? Ninety percent of people in the United States have prayed for another person's healing (Levin 2016). Likely, the global estimates are similar. But do prayers and healing thoughts actually do anything?

In fact, they do. People sending positive healing intentions from a distance or without physical contact have a small but consistent positive effect. These positive results are also seen when the intentions were sent to nonhuman animals, cells, or plants (Roe, Sonnex, and Roxburgh 2015).[18] Modalities like Therapeutic Touch, Reiki, and spiritual healing for conditions including pain, cancer, mental health symptoms, and hypertension have positive research results (Rao et al. 2016; Jain et al. 2015; Yount et al. 2021). These results are extraordinary because we would expect the effect of noncontact healing to be zero! Clearly, something is going on.

These are all examples of channeling experiences that affect our physical world. At their core is human intention. Your directed and unconscious intention matters. It can affect objects. People can tell when you direct it at them. Your intentions affect other people's bodies. The effects of our intentions can be instantaneous and do not depend on distance. These results are remarkable.

The body of evidence I've just described is not made up. It is the combined effort of thousands of people and decades' worth of rigorous research. True, the effects are often small. However, they are still apparent and can be measured. You can use this information to feel confident when you get the dreaded questions asking if channeling is real.

But wait, there is more.

Knowing Things We Shouldn't Know

You can also learn information about the world that you couldn't possibly know through only your traditional five senses. The most common term for this is extrasensory perception—the ability to perceive beyond our senses. It is also called anomalous cognition and receptive psi. It includes things like telepathy, clairvoyance, precognition, and mediumship. Let's review what we know about the "realness" of these types of channeling experiences.

Mind-to-Mind Communication

One day, I was sitting quietly during my morning meditation. Suddenly, I saw a picture of my mother and knew that something was wrong. I finished my meditation and called her. She started laughing through tears. She was distraught, thanked me for calling, and said she had just been thinking about me and was going to call. She just learned some alarming news about a family member and needed support to process it.

People all over the world experience mind-to-mind communication or telepathic experiences like this every day. Your friend might bring up some obscure memory or topic that you had just been thinking about. Your phone rings, and you know who is calling you.

Believe it or not, there is such a thing as telephone telepathy. People all over the globe have participated in telephone telepathy experiments (Sheldrake 2015). They sign up to guess who is calling them (without a caller ID system, of course). None of the volunteers are right all the time, but they were correct more than what would have been expected by chance. When a familiar person was calling them, their correct guesses doubled. Positive telepathy has even been found using emails and text messages!

There is a unique technique called "ganzfeld" that improves people's telepathic ability. The ganzfeld technique was initially developed in the 1930s in the experimental psychology field. It is used to reduce input from our senses. The idea was that reducing input from the outside world would allow telepathy to happen more easily (Bem 1993; Braud, Wood, and Braud 1975).

Imagine arriving at an experimental research laboratory with a friend. You are the "sender," and your friend is the "receiver." You go into separate soundproof rooms for a thirty-minute session. The experimenter gives you a picture of a field full of pink and yellow tulips with a blue sky and puffy white clouds. The experimenter then tells you to focus on the image and "send" it to your friend.

At the same time, your friend is in another room. They are sitting in a reclining chair. They have translucent ping-pong ball halves taped over their eyes and headphones over their ears. Another experimenter guides them through a progressive relaxation process to relax their body. A red floodlight is directed toward their eyes. The red light through the ping-pong balls creates a homogenous visual field over the eyes. This means that what they see is the same everywhere. What they hear is the same everywhere also because white noise, like what you might hear listening to a waterfall, is played through their headphones. Because what your friend is seeing and hearing is unchanging, the internal "noise" their body receives is reduced (Bem, Palmer, and Broughton 2001).

For a thirty-minute session, you "send" an image to your friend, and they share what they mentally see or think with the researcher. Your friend then has to choose one of four images that they think you sent to them.

This ganzfeld protocol has been used for decades to see if it boosts telepathy. Numerous studies show that it does (Baptista, Derakhshani, and Tressoldi 2015; Cardeña 2018; Storm, Tressoldi, and Di Risio 2010). Ganzfeld telepathy study results are some of the most reliable and robust findings in parapsychology. It is mind-boggling to think that all the sensory input we receive might be blocking our ability to communicate with our mind. Maybe that is why most channelers practice some type of meditation or other practice to quiet their mind.

You can also experience different types of telepathy. Many people experience channeling, not in their waking life, but while they sleep. Dream-ESP is a form of extrasensory perception that happens while dreaming. Dream-ESP studies are also among the most evidential and long-standing research programs on channeling.

Dream-ESP studies are like the ganzfeld studies with a sender and a receiver. Unlike in the ganzfeld studies, the receiver is asleep. The receiver is connected to physical measuring devices and goes to sleep in the laboratory. The experimenter then "sends" an image into the receiver's dreams. When the receiver wakes up, they share their dreams with a staff member who didn't see the image (Krippner 2005). More than twenty-five years of dream-ESP studies and follow-up research show that dreamers dreamt about and correctly identified the targets more often than we would expect by chance (Storm and Rock 2015; Storm et al. 2017).

You've read about telepathy through the telephone, emails, and texts, and while awake and asleep. There are even studies showing telepathy with animals too! Extensive research shows that some animals can sense things about their owners beyond their usual ways of knowing. Thousands of case histories collected from around the world show animals that appeared to have telepathy with their owners (Sheldrake 2015). Seeing telepathy between animals and humans is helpful because we can't imagine how the animals could be making it up or cheating.

Have you ever experienced mind-to-mind communication? Reflect on any telepathic experience you have had or heard about. Notice if any specific conditions could have allowed the communication to happen. Were there any emotions involved? How far away were the people from each other? What else did you notice about the experience?

Mind-to-mind communication has been shown over and over again in different settings. This is one area of research that is developed and robust. You can put this into your pocket to support you in those "But, is channeling real?" conversations. Perhaps telepathy isn't so much science fiction but a documentary.

Seeing What We Shouldn't See

Did you see the 2009 movie *Men Who Stare at Goats*? It was a fictional depiction based on a true story—a twenty-year United States secret government psychic program. Star Gate was the most extensive funded program in parapsychology, receiving approximately $20 million from 1972 to 1995. The secret program is not so secret anymore. The release of previously confidential governmental documents allowed the program to come into the light.

Remote viewing was a regular activity the soldiers did. Remote viewing is a usually structured practice of seeking impressions about a distant or unseen target that someone would not be able to usually know. Remote viewing is a type of clairvoyance, although the name "remote viewing" has less stigma associated with it.

Drs. May and Marwaha synthesized all the Star Gate material in a comprehensive four-volume text. They commented on the remote viewing results: "In a total of 504 separate missions from 1973–1995, remote viewing produced actionable intelligence prompting 89 percent of the customers to return with additional missions. The Star Gate data indicates that informational psi is a scientifically valid phenomenon" (May and Marwaha 2018a, 2018b).[19]

Other formal remote viewing meta-analyses report some of the most substantial effects in parapsychology (Baptista, Derakhshani, and Tressoldi 2015; Cardeña 2018; Dunne and Jahn 2003; Milton 1997).[20] Dr. Russel Targ (2019), another key player in remote viewing programs, shared that many of his experiments showed results *four times* what you would expect by chance. He said, "The accuracy and reliability of remote viewing is independent of distance up to 10,000 km, and of time up to several days into the future" (569). Again, we see this notion of nonlocality. In the case of remote viewing, people's consciousness can go beyond time and space to see places, people, and so forth from afar and even in the future.

Remote viewing is used for many practical applications, not just militaristic ones. It is also used for the stock market, futures or other financial market information, sport event outcomes, locations of missing persons or criminal cases, and finding unknown archaeological sites (Schwartz, De Mattei, and Smith 2019; Schwartz 2019; Kolodziejzyk 2013). It can also be easily tested in the laboratory with rigorous methods.[21]

A structured remote viewing session would go something like this: You are the remote viewer. You call your manager, who gives you a six-digit number, such as 987-513. You then connect with whatever will be associated with that "target" in the future. You then share with your manager a detailed description of your impressions. After all the impressions are turned in, your manager randomly chooses two pictures from a large set of images. One of those pictures is randomly assigned to represent the S&P 500 going up and the other, the S&P 500 going down. A judge reviews all the remote viewer impressions to see how closely they match the S&P 500 going-up picture or the S&P 500 going-down picture. If the judges' ratings show a strong match, then the S&P 500 trade would be made for that direction. For example, the image representing the S&P 500 going up had a red balloon on an orange background, and the picture representing the S&P 500 going down had a blue boat on the ocean. If all the remote viewers mentioned the colors red and orange and a round object, that would indicate the S&P 500 going up. This is just one example of how remote viewing is used for practical applications. And people have made money this way, showing that it works (Smith, Laham, and Moddel 2014; Harary and Targ 1985)!

I firmly believe practical applications of channeling like this are what will drive the loosening of taboos. Laboratory evidence doesn't seem to impress people as much as practical applications do. Especially if it makes them money!

Knowing the Future

Being able to know what will happen in the future can indeed be practical. Premonitions have been documented throughout history (Dossey 2009). Premonitions, predictions, prophecies, precognition…all have to do with knowing the future.

Precognition, like telepathy, also happens in dreams. Dream-ESP studies found the same positive results if the image was chosen before or after dreaming. This means that the dreamer knew about the image if it was picked in the future. Incredible, right? Some of the earliest channeling researchers talk about precognition and dreams. Late nineteenth-century researcher Eleanor M. Sidgwick looked at precognition that happened outside of a laboratory. She noticed that precognition showed up as visions, auditory impressions, and in about two-thirds of the time, as dreams (Alvarado 2008). Fewer formal precognitive dream studies have been done in the laboratory. There are some studies, but there aren't enough to say that "dreams can reveal the content of upcoming unpredictable events" (Mossbridge and Radin 2017).

Waking precognition has been extensively studied in the laboratory. The forced-choice task I mentioned in chapter 3 can also be designed as a precognition experiment. That is the one where you pick which of five symbols will show up on the screen next. If the computer randomly selects the symbol *after* you pick which one you think will show up on the screen next, then it is a precognition task rather than a clairvoyance task. Hundreds of "forced-choice" precognitive experiments have been conducted over the last century. When we combine all of these results, we see that people can guess what will show up in the future more than they would by chance (Storm, Tressoldi, and Di Risio 2010; Honorton, Ferrari, and Hansen 2018).

Forced-choice tests aren't used as much today. They are easy to do, but people become bored with the task very quickly. They also don't really reflect how people experience precognition in their daily lives (Baptista, Derakhshani, and Tressoldi 2015; Cardeña 2018; Storm, Tressoldi, and Di Risio 2010; Honorton, Ferrari, and Hansen 2018).

Many researchers have moved to free-response precognitive tasks. In free-response tasks, the person can describe what they think the target in the future will be rather than being forced to choose one of many options. Reviews of free-response studies over forty-four years of research also show that people can describe a future target more than expected by chance (Mossbridge and Radin 2017; Storm and Tressoldi 2020).

In the studies you've seen in this section so far, the people know they are guessing what will come in the future. But what about experiments where people don't know that is what is being measured? Implicit precognition refers to just that. In implicit precognition, you see that people's actions in the present change based on something that happens in the future.

Implicit precognition was made famous by Cornell University Professor Daryl Bem, who published his controversial results in 2011. They were controversial because he took a commonly used psychology task and turned it on its head.

In the classical task, a person sees a screen with a *word* on it, like "happy" or "sad." On the next screen, they see a happy or sad *image*. This is called priming. The person is being primed by the word before they view the image. The person's job is to press a 1 if the picture is happy or a 0 if the picture is sad as fast as they can. People press the button more quickly if "happy" comes before the happy image of rainbows (congruent). People are slower when they don't match—when, for example, "happy" comes before a sad picture of a little girl crying (incongruent).

Dr. Bem created a big stir because his participants got the congruent-incongruent effect on speed if the word came *after* the picture rather than *before*. This is incredible. This means that how fast the person pressed a button was affected by a word that showed up *after* they pressed the button. Other researchers got similar results. Combining ninety studies of Bem's task showed a precognition effect overall.[22] These results were spotlighted in the media because they were about a well-known psychology test and because Dr. Bem was from Cornell University. The controversy over these results still continues (Ritchie, Wiseman, and French 2012; Galak et al. 2012).

Our Bodies Know Before We Do

In the remote staring studies, you saw that many people noticed sensations in their bodies, making them turn to the "looker." Sometimes there was tingling or warmth or a sense of wrongness. People's bodies were also sensitive in the sender-receiver studies you saw. This can happen outside of the laboratory when there isn't a specific person sending the information. Sometimes your body feels something in your everyday life without your mind knowing. The body seems to have its own sensitivity or sense of knowingness that can tell us about the future.

Precognition that you learned about in the last section is about knowing something about the future, or a preknowing. On the other hand, presentiment is about feeling or accessing information in the body before something happens in linear time, and usually in an unconscious way. Presentiment is a *prefeeling* (Radin and Pierce 2015). For example, some studies have shown that people's heart rate and eye pupil dilation have reacted to something in the future without them knowing what was coming. Here's a presentiment example from one of our studies:

I was sitting at a traffic light, with my infant daughter asleep in the back. I noticed the couple in the car to my right, talking happily. Our light turned green. Everything felt wrong. I hesitated, and at that time, the couple next to me who had pulled forward was T-boned by another car. It would have been me.

This person's physical response saved their and their daughter's life. They did not get a vision of a crash or a mental knowingness to stop. They felt it in their body, which caused a hesitation, which prevented them from being in the accident.

Presentiment laboratory studies tell us that our bodies react to randomly delivered information approximately one to ten seconds *in the future* (Mossbridge, Tressoldi, and Utts 2012; Mossbridge et al. 2014). Interestingly, erotic and negative images produce stronger responses in our body compared to emotionally neutral pictures. The body's response before the image is the same as it would typically respond after seeing it. For example, if the future image is an erotic one, the body would be more aroused *before* the erotic picture. Dr. Mossbridge summarizes, presentiment "has been under investigation for more than three decades, and a recent conservative meta-analysis suggests that the phenomenon is real." Other reviews corroborate this, expressing that presentiment is a genuine and repeatable phenomenon (Mossbridge and Radin 2017; Mossbridge et al. 2014; Mossbridge, Tressoldi, and Utts 2012).

These studies are incredible. In Western culture, we are very head oriented. Training to be present and listen to our body is rare. The West's increase in mindfulness has helped shift this, but we still have a long way to go. There is clearly more wisdom that we can glean by listening to our body.

Have you ever had an experience where your body gave you the information you needed? Were you able to hear it? Do you regularly listen to the messages your body is giving you?

Perhaps you can cultivate your capacity for listening to your body's prefeelings to help you make wiser decisions. We'll talk about this and other ways to nurture our channeling in a later chapter.

Knowing Beyond Death

A distant cousin of mine had just died of colon cancer. Laila was forty-six years old, married, and had young children. Her deeply spiritual family was devastated. They couldn't understand how it could possibly be her time to go. They decided to reach out to a medium to see if they could connect with her. They had an emotional session. They felt the medium was connecting with Laila because of the very specific and personal messages they received. After the session, they were still in grief but were comforted because they received answers about why she passed so young. It helped them move on with their grieving process. This is just one of many stories about mediumship supporting people with grief (Beischel, Mosher, and Boccuzzi 2015).

Mental mediums report that they communicate with deceased human beings or other discarnate entities *mentally*. This is different from trance channelers who believe the spirit is using their body to communicate directly.[23] But is mediumship real? Can mediums get accurate information about deceased people that they wouldn't know otherwise? We may never know if mental mediums are actually contacting deceased humans or tapping into some telepathic reservoir of knowledge (Rock, Beischel, and Cott 2009; Beischel and Rock 2009). We can, however, check if the information they receive is correct.

Drs. Julie Beischel and Mark Boccuzzi at the Windbridge Research Center have championed mediumship research, outreach, and education. Their research center tagline is "Studying dying, death, and what comes next." Their and others' laboratory studies show that mediums can receive accurate and specific information about deceased individuals. The strictest methods are used to prevent the mediums from learning information through cues from the person getting the reading, prior knowledge of the deceased person, or other deceptive tactics (Beischel and Schwartz 2007; Beischel et al. 2015; Delorme et al. 2013). Volumes have been written describing tests of the validity of mediumship in and out of the laboratory (Rock et al. 2020; Sarraf, Woodley, and Tressoldi 2020; Braude 2003; Fontana 2005).

Dr. Arnaud Delorme heads up the mediumship studies at our lab. In one study, Dr. Delorme asked twelve mediums to look at photos of people's faces. The mediums had to choose whether the person was alive or deceased.

Overall, the mediums were accurate more than expected by chance (Delorme et al. 2018). In a follow-up study, twelve professional mediums and twelve people without mediumship abilities looked at photos of people's faces. This time, they chose how the person died. There were three choices: heart attack, death by firearm, or car accident. All the people grouped together guessed better than expected by chance. In fact, the people who said they did not have mediumship abilities did better on the task than the mediums (Delorme et al. 2020).

There could be many reasons why this was true. Perhaps we all get information in nontraditional ways, even if we don't think we do. Maybe the mediums were not performing at their best. The mediums said they felt some performance anxiety about the task since it differed from their usual way of doing readings. Their heart rates were higher during the task compared to the other participants. They also said they wouldn't normally "tune in" to 201 photographs so quickly. We wondered if they would do better at home without time pressure and the stress of the lab. We emailed the same mediums fifteen random images they hadn't seen before (different ones for each medium). They could take their time to choose how the person died. The mediums did do better on the at-home task than they did in the lab. Many of them gave extensive notes about each person, which were accurate.

So can we say that every medium is accurate every time? No. Sometimes this leads people to discount all mediums. However, the idea that some mediums can provide verified information about deceased people is now well supported by evidence. More process-oriented rather than proof-oriented studies will help us learn a lot more about mediumship and understand how and when mediums can be more accurate.

Fewer formal studies have looked at the accuracy of trance channeled information. Trance channelers have produced volumes of material on just about everything including the sciences, music, art, literary creations, health diagnosis and treatment, religion and psychology, gardening, and community. There are a few studies that have tested the accuracy of some trance channeled information. Still, much of it has not been formally evaluated.

One study looked at channeled material from the automatic writing of Chico Xavier, a very prolific and influential channeler in Brazil. They found ninety-nine items of verifiable information, and 98 percent of these items were rated as "clear and precise fit." No item was rated as "no fit" (Rocha et al. 2014).

Stephan Schwartz (2005) shares verified cases in his book *The Secret Vaults of Time*. One example is Frederick Bligh Bond and Captain John Allen Bartlett, who channeled together using automatic writing. They believed they were channeling the monks who lived at Glastonbury. With the information they received, Bond was able to successfully excavate the Glastonbury Cathedral and Abbey. There are numerous other amazing archaeological stories where channelers find sites and describe events from the distant past (in linear time).

The Challenger Research Project is another example.[24] The Space Shuttle Challenger exploded on January 28, 1986, shortly after its launch. I vividly remember watching that launch myself. I was on pins and needles watching the rocket take off. I was excited and somewhat nervous because I couldn't imagine what it would feel like to be one of those astronauts.

Then it exploded. I felt shock, disbelief, and then a deep sadness for the astronauts and their families. Channeler Jeanne Love believes she has channeled the Challenger astronauts. The channeled material includes specific details about what happened in the shuttle and how they died. According to Jeanne, most astronauts drowned afterward rather than in the explosion. This information was contrary to the news at the time. Only later did NASA confirm that this was true. Jeanne described other details, such as the cause of the explosion, the politics of NASA at the time, and information on a payload designed to test aspects of the Strategic Defense Initiative. These details were not public information when channeled, and many have since been disclosed and verified.

Is Channeling Real?

This chapter has briefly summarized the vast amount of evidence available on the "realness" of channeling. There have literally been thousands and thousands of pages written on this topic. It is challenging to give this topic justice in a single chapter. I invite you to think of this chapter as an introduction to verifiable evidence. Hopefully, it will inspire your curiosity to continue learning.

How does this evidence change your perceptions about whether channeling is real or not? What ways do you think channeling should be studied to verify the information received?

I find it hard to believe that anyone could read through the voluminous research that I just briefly summarized and still say that channeling doesn't exist.

Yes, for many channeling types, the effects are small. Perhaps we'll find some other explanation for the effects. I've also left out many nuances to these channeling effects that are far beyond this book's scope. However, affecting the world with your mind and knowing things you would normally have no way of knowing do happen. They can be measured in the laboratory under controlled conditions. They are indeed happening spontaneously in dreams and in people's daily lives.

Advice for Talking About Channeling

What about all those people who say that it is impossible or that there is no evidence? I want to jump up and down and say, "There is, there is!" Talking to someone who is curious or skeptical can be challenging. When I am confronted by someone asking if channeling is real, I first try to engage them in a conversation. Conversations often open doors to understanding. Engagement is much more useful than convincing, which tends to push people away. This is especially true if channeling doesn't fit within their current world view.

I will often begin by asking, "Do you think they are real?" I will then ask, "Have you or someone you know had a channeling experience?" Usually, these two questions go a long way toward creating a conversation. Sometimes people are very ingrained in their beliefs that it can't possibly exist. That is okay. They have a right to their opinion, and I don't try to change it. I kindly change the topic and move on to something else. I also lovingly imagine that they might have a direct experience of it themselves in the future.

I can talk myself blue in the face about the evidence from this study and that study. Science alone isn't a panacea to open people's minds. Suppose a person doesn't believe in channeling. In that case, they likely won't change their mind despite all the extraordinary evidence I can show them. They often need a direct firsthand experience of it themselves to become open and curious about channeling—I find science plus direct experience is the best combination. Science can help someone who has not had an experience to open to the possibility. Science gives context to someone who has.

I know it is crucial for many people in our Western culture to see the "proof." However, I think the most important discoveries about channeling lie in how it works and how you can use it to support your daily life.

CHAPTER 5

How Does Channeling Work?

I was one of those children who was incessantly asking questions. How does our car engine work? Where does rain come from? How do airplanes stay up? I had an insatiable curiosity focused mostly on the mechanisms of how things worked. I loved taking things apart and trying to figure out how to put them back together. I imagine you too have a natural curiosity for how things work.

If you ask me the simple question, "How does channeling work?" I can begin with the most simplistic answer at this moment: "We don't know." When I first launched the channeling research program, I had the naïve hope that there would be one solution to the puzzle of how channeling works. What I realize now is that there are likely many ways that channeling works, and that those ways are probably dependent upon the person doing the channeling and the type of information they are revealing.

For some of us, understanding how something works helps give us context for our experiences. It can allow others to be more open to the experience and reduce fear and anxiety. Airplane turbulence is an example. My anxiety about turbulence became so intense after 9/11 that I was afraid to fly. I spoke to a pilot friend who explained that turbulence is caused by changes in airflow. He told me to imagine myself in a car on a bumpy road. Having the information about what caused turbulence dramatically reduced my fear and anxiety about flying. I was still uncomfortable when the plane bounced around, but I was better able to manage my emotions knowing the cause.

While we don't know precisely how channeling works, we have learned a great deal about it over the last century. Several theories have been proposed. Reviewing all the theories and their nuances is beyond this book's scope, but I want to give you an overview of some of the main ones.[25] You'll notice as you review them that some of the theories are relevant to some channeling types more than others.

Channeling Doesn't Work Through Force

You saw much evidence for psychokinesis, or how our consciousness affects the physical world, in the last chapters. But how does our consciousness actually influence the world? Is there some force that is emitted from us that causes a change elsewhere in the world? Hollywood has shown us creative visuals for what force-like energy could look like. Visualize Doctor Strange with the glowing orange lines of light emanating from his hands. He uses those to ward off the villains or create a shield. Some would think that there is a force-like agent coming from our minds or bodies that is creating the physical change in the environment. If channeling worked by some sort of force, it would depend on physical laws that the material world is constrained by: time flows in a linear forward direction, and traveling distances in space requires time. But space and time do not always affect channeling experiments, and our choices and desires do! From these results, we are pretty sure that channeling does not work via some sort of force.

Channeling Transcends Space and Time

One way we know that space does not matter in channeling is by looking at the random number generator (RNG) studies we talked about in the last chapter. The Princeton Engineering Anomalies Research Laboratory collected RNG data for six years (Dunne and Jahn 1992). People worldwide directed their intention toward the RNGs from one to nine thousand miles away from the lab. The person's distance from the RNG did not change the results. The results from a person who was nine thousand miles away were the same as from a person sitting right in front of the RNG (Varvoglis and Bancel 2015). This means that the ability for your intention to affect the physical world (in this case, the RNG) does not depend on space. A beam of energy's strength would decrease the farther away the person was from the RNG. But because we don't see this effect of distance, it tells us that beams of energy zapping out of people's minds are not what affect the RNGs. The twenty-year Global Consciousness Project found similar results (Nelson 2015).

So did the sender-receiver studies (also called DMILS, direct mental interactions with living systems) I mentioned in the last chapter. Distance does not matter. These studies support the notion that your consciousness is not limited by space.

Time also does not matter. We know that time is not absolute from Einstein's theory of general relativity. We can imagine how this could be true for astronauts. The time elapsed for an astronaut traveling to Mars is different from the time elapsed on Earth. But for the average person, time appears to move linearly and in a forward direction. This is not so with channeling phenomenon.

RNG studies also found that the specific time that people direct their intention to the RNG does not influence the results (Varvoglis and Bancel 2015). A person can direct their intention to data from the past or the future and affect the data. In the DMILS studies, the sender's intention on the receiver was instantaneous. If our intentions were a force coming out of our minds to influence the physical world, then it would take some time for that force to travel to what we were trying to affect. The fact that senders can affect the receivers' bodies instantaneously and that senders can influence data in the past or future supports the notion that our intentions are not some physical force.

Channeling Works Because Everything Is Interconnected

But how can we possibly affect and know things in the past or future or things that are far away from us? This idea is in stark contrast to the prevailing notion that consciousness is a product of our brain. Our current model for how the world works is based on a materialistic paradigm. Materialism promotes the view that nothing exists except matter and its movements and changes. That is why it might seem strange to you that you could affect things with your intention at a distance.

Whether the brain generates consciousness or acts as an antenna or receiver for consciousness is a hugely debated topic. What if our consciousness were not limited to our physical brain? We could potentially receive information from any time and any space. This notion, which I mentioned in chapter 1, is called nonlocal consciousness, which means our consciousness is not limited by our conventional ideas of time and space.

You have seen the reality of this statement over and over again in the laboratory studies' results. Experiments in physics now provide some background for how these results could be so.

Big bang cosmology, or the study of the origin and development of the Universe, tells us that there was a point in time where everything in the Universe was connected (Buniy and Hsu 2012). In theory, this means that the physical properties of a photon at one end of the Universe are completely linked to another photon at the other end of the Universe. The physical properties of the photons, like position, speed, and spin, are connected. For example, suppose you change the spin of one entangled photon. In that case, the paired photon's spin will also change *instantaneously* and *across long distances*. This relationship between quantum systems is called quantum entanglement.

Einstein called this "spooky action at a distance" partly because these actions do not follow classical physics rules (Born 1971, 158). The relationship or correlation between the two photons has been repeatedly confirmed in laboratories in up to eight photons (Yao et al. 2012). Quantum entanglement can also be seen in photon pairs from two distant, ancient quasars emitted 7.8 billion years ago and 12.2 billion years ago (Rauch et al. 2018).

These results are not limited to photons. Entanglement is even seen in small molecules called buckyballs and even macroscopic diamonds! The implications of these experiments are mind-blowing. Labs worldwide are rushing to implement practical applications like quantum information and computation systems (Bub 2019). Suppose every single thing in the Universe were connected. In that case, we begin to get a glimpse of how channeling could potentially work and how you can affect things halfway across the world with your intentions.

Channeling Is a Result of Our Consciousness Being Fundamental

Let's take this line of thinking one step further. You already saw that channeling doesn't work in a force-like way that you see in classical physics. It works in a quantum physics way—nonlocally. You read about multiple experiments where people know and affect things in ways that go beyond our usual ways of knowing and conventional notions of time and space. If channeling works nonlocally, then what is the explanation for how that happens?

Cosmologist Jude Currivan says information is the explanation. In her recent book, *The Cosmic Hologram: In-Formation at the Center of Creation*, Dr. Currivan provides evidence that reconciles quantum mechanics and classical physics. She shows that energy-matter and space-time are complementary expressions of information. In fact, she supports the notion that our Universe is an interconnected hologram of information. And that consciousness is the fundamental nature of who we are (Currivan 2017). That consciousness, of which our consciousness is one small part, is what the Universe is.

This notion supposes that consciousness pervades the Universe and is fundamental (and not the product of our brain). Consciousness being fundamental also assumes that everything material arises out of consciousness. The concept of consciousness as fundamental is gaining support and evidence in many scientific circles (Cook 2020; Goff 2019; Chalmers 1996).

Dr. Currivan explains these ideas through detailed arguments. Here are a few highlights of her views: Information is the fundamental nature of reality and the ultimate unity of consciousness. Because of this, your human consciousness is not limited to your physical brain or body. Your consciousness can also go beyond our conventional notions of space and time. These nonlocal connections are a natural part of the entire Universe and allow the Universe to evolve as a single united whole. Within this whole, there is no separation of time and space. What one part of the Universe "knows," the rest of the Universe spontaneously "knows."

Before something is observed or measured, all possible outcomes exist simultaneously, and space and time are nonlocally connected. It is only through the observation or measurement that any one outcome becomes a "reality." So, unless the measurement is set up to observe the nonlocal connection between *all* the outcomes, only one specific outcome will be observed; that is, it will only appear that there is one outcome. In your day-to-day life, that one outcome becomes what you call "reality." However, this is just one aspect of what our Universe truly is.

Dr. Currivan highlights the implications of what this means, saying that we are both the manifestations and co-creators of our reality. Basically, the Universe's consciousness, of which your consciousness is a part, co-creates the reality you see around you.

Channeling Is You Creating Your Reality

Consciousness is fundamental. Co-creating our reality. This sounds like science fiction. First, I say that your consciousness goes beyond time and space, and now I'm saying you create our reality! I know it sounds fantastic. The details of how cosmology and physics show this to be true are far outside this book's scope. Let's see if I can bring it closer to you with other theories and evidence for how channeling works.

You saw that time and space aren't at play in intention studies. This goes a long way in supporting the idea that channeling doesn't work through some force or classical physics. Interestingly, it also lines up with the idea of you co-creating your reality through your behaviors and choices.

Decision augmentation theory (DAT) says your choices influence outcomes. DAT proposes that you are continuously and unconsciously accessing information from the past, present, and future. With this information, you are then making decisions or selecting information that results in the outcome you expect or desire.

For example, imagine laboratory experiments where a participant presses a button to start a trial. According to DAT, they are (unconsciously) pressing the button at the exact right moment to produce the results that they or the experimenter wants to see. The simplest way to think about this is that your effect on the physical world is not a force but a way of "seeing" the information (Varvoglis and Bancel 2015). Essentially, your behavior creates your reality.

Goal-directed effects also support the notion that you are a co-creator of your reality. When the feedback a person gets in a task drives the results, the effects are goal-directed. The person's goal to increase a red light happens regardless of what calculations are happening on the back end.

For example, if the person's goal is to increase the red light and the red light is connected to more 1s for the RNG, then there will be more 1s. If the person's goal is to increase the red light, but the red light is connected to more 0s for the RNG, then there will be more 0s. It doesn't matter what the back-end analysis is. The person is creating the result they want—in this case, more red light. The person's goal determines the outcome, regardless of how or what it takes to get there.

This example with the red light and more 1s or 0s is straightforward. Goal-directed effects even happen with many steps on the back end to increase the red light, meaning it doesn't matter how many steps there are; you get the results you are focused on getting (Kennedy 1995; Radin 2006; Schmidt 1987). Imagine the world in which you envision the outcome you want, and the Universe conspires to provide you that outcome. The implications of the DAT and goal-oriented theory are astounding.

This concept of consciousness as fundamental, as being information-driven, and that we co-create it is supported by cosmology, quantum physics, and experiments in the laboratory. Imagine almost eight billion people on our planet with their conscious and unconscious goals being projected simultaneously. You have your conscious desires mixed in with your unconscious desires that support some outcome. But then your neighbor might have the complete opposite. What is the result in this case? Maybe what we are seeing in the world today is a vast combination of all of our unconscious and unconscious goals—definitely something to think about.

Unconscious Channeling Drives Your Everyday Choices

Okay, you know that our behaviors and goals can influence experimental results in the laboratory. But what about in everyday life? Do these theories about how channeling works apply to our daily lives? You make hundreds of little choices each day. Each of those choices adds up to create the experience of your day. What happens when you decide to take the country road home rather than the freeway? Or choose to go to this restaurant instead of that one? Or decide to work at home on Thursday instead of Wednesday? Each of those decisions changes your experienced life.

One day I was running late for work. It was my usual time to leave, but I decided to do one last thing. I started driving about thirty minutes after I would usually have. Later, I learned that there was a seven-car pile-up on the freeway in the general area I would have been if I had left at my usual time. I could have been in the accident. Was there an unconscious process that made me late? Did my unconscious know about the future accident and use that to protect me? Supporters of the psi-mediated instrumental response (PMIR) model and first-sight model and theory (FSMT) would probably say yes.

PMIR is a model for channeling experiences that happen spontaneously in daily life. It proposes that people unconsciously get information that is relevant to what they need. They then unconsciously use this information to modify their behavior to meet their needs (Stanford 2015), just like I was unconsciously late and avoided a car accident. PMIR refers to the psychological ways that channeling might function in a person's life that serves their inherent qualities of mind and character and needs. It basically says that you use channeling without any conscious effort or awareness that it is even happening.

Similarly, the first-sight model and theory (FSMT) proposes that it is in your essential nature to participate actively, all the time, and unconsciously in your world. And that your world is much larger in time and space than your immediate boundaries. All of your experiences and behaviors result from unconscious psychological processes that are acted out based on multiple sources of information, including those beyond your traditional five senses (Carpenter, n.d.). FSMT proposes that channeling is not an ability that needs to be nurtured or trained or coaxed into working but an innate universal characteristic of all living organisms.

Reflect upon your channeling experiences. Did they give you firsthand evidence for channeling being nonlocal? How does the concept that consciousness is fundamental change how you view the world? Imagine that the idea that you co-create your reality is true. Would that change how you behave or relate to others?

Hollywood special effects are incredible. The red beams coming out of the Scarlet Witch's eyes and hands or Captain Marvel's white eyes in *The Avengers* are meant to be just that, incredible. They are meant to visually show us something. Our consciousness's effect on the physical world likely doesn't happen with some force-like energy or beam in real life. It transcends time and space and is probably driven by our behaviors and choices motivated by our goals and desires, conscious and unconscious.

Your Natural Channeling Is Blocked by Something

So if channeling is an innate universal characteristic and you are a co-creator of your reality, why aren't you always having channeling experiences? Why doesn't you thinking, *What is [fill in the blank] thinking right now?* allow you to immediately know what they are thinking?

Imagine that there is an infinite amount of information and sensory input that you could potentially take in. And that you are already accessing that information from beyond time and space. However, the information is jumbled or is hidden or blocked in some way. Some theorize that perhaps our innate channeling ability is blocked by other external signals that our traditional five senses receive. As you already saw in the last chapter, some researchers tested the ganzfeld technique for telepathy with remarkably positive results (Bem 1993; Braud, Wood, and Braud 1975; Bem, Palmer, and Broughton 2001; Baptista, Derakhshani, and Tressoldi 2015). Perhaps you are just bombarded by other signals and overlook the extrasensory information. The ganzfeld experiment results certainly support this idea.

Another idea is that your brain acts as a gatekeeper to slow down or filter the infinite amount of information you have access to. This would be a defense mechanism so you aren't overwhelmed by what would feel like a fire hydrant rush of water. Channeling happens when the filter is reduced or changed somehow to allow more information to arise than you would typically have access to (Luke 2015). Studies where people take psychedelics and researchers measure their brain chemistry and function support this theory.[26]

Imagine that you've enrolled in a psilocybin mushroom study. You take the mushrooms in a safe and controlled environment. During your trip, the blood flow in your brain is measured. When the researcher looked at your and others' brain results, they found that blood flow was reduced! That is contrary to what most would think. Most mushroom trippers would guess that their brain was more active during the trip. They usually see vibrant colors and feel increased sensations. The reduction in blood flow was especially true in a brain area related to our sense of separateness and identity. The author summarized the results quite nicely: "These results strongly imply that the subjective effects of psychedelic drugs are caused by decreased activity and connectivity in the brain's key connector hubs, enabling a state of unconstrained cognition" (Carhart-Harris et al. 2012).

Unconstrained cognition sounds a lot like many channeling experiences. Why would psychedelic studies have anything to do with channeling experiences? Many of the states experienced during psychedelic "trips" are like channeling states. More spontaneous channeling was reported with people on psychedelics, like mescaline, LSD, psilocybin, ayahuasca, and cannabis. Overall, people on psychedelics do better on psi tasks than people who are not when they can respond freely (rather than being forced to choose one out of multiple answers; Luke 2015).

Ketamine is another drug that has been studied in relation to channeling. Ketamine is generally used for anesthesia and creates feelings of being disconnected from oneself. Ketamine also causes experiences of telepathy, precognition, clairvoyance, psychokinesis, communication with the dead, and increased synchronicities (Luke 2012).

Perhaps psychedelics influence brain chemistry to lessen your channeling filter. In this way, they allow more information in, and so you have more channeling experiences. These studies show that perhaps something is blocking your ability to fully know the entirety of our interconnectedness.

If you have taken psychedelics in your life, reflect on how the experience was for you. Does the idea that our natural channeling ability is blocked by some protective mechanism resonate with you? How do you imagine we could strengthen our natural channeling ability without being overwhelmed by stimuli?

I can't imagine perceiving everything in the Universe right now. My human mind just couldn't process it all. I would be completely overwhelmed and not be able to function. Perhaps there are filters to channeling built in to protect us in some way from the enormity of our true nature.

Your Body as Your Channeling Instrument

Even if we prove entirely that we are all interconnected, that consciousness is fundamental and nonlocal, that we are co-creators of our reality, and that we are intrinsically connected to everything in an informational Universe, the fact remains that we currently exist in a human body. Some interface must exist between the Universe and your human body to process the information or act upon your environment.

One large area of research studies this interface by looking at channeling and physiological correlates. Physiological correlates are measurable in the body, like body chemicals, brain waves, heart waves, and skin temperature, and are connected to psychological or other states. We are not sure if the body changes are directly associated with how channeling works. But it does tell us about how our bodies relate to the states. We don't exactly know how the channeling-body interface works, but have learned much through studies on brain, chemical, and electrical signals in the body and the pineal gland.

Nervous System Chemicals and Hormones Change with Channeling

Neurotransmitters and hormones are chemicals in the body responsible for communication in our nervous system and the rest of our body, respectively. Many studies have been done to see how these change during channeling experiences.

Norie Kawai and a team of researchers developed a relationship of mutual trust with indigenous groups in Bali over twenty years. This allowed them to collect fifteen people's blood before and after a sacred ritual drama called Calonarang and test for neurotransmitters (Kawai et al. 2001). Calonarang is performed at midnight in the garden of a Balinese temple. The ritual drama enacts warriors who are believed to be possessed by evil spirits through a witch's power. Three neurotransmitters were higher in people who were in a trance during the drama compared to people who were moving in similar ways but were not in a trance. The same researchers found differences in brain wave activity in a study sixteen years later (Kawai et al. 2017). Other researchers have looked at other blood hormones with mixed results (Bastos, Bastos, dos Santos, et al. 2018; Beischel, Tassone, and Boccuzzi 2019).

Electrical Signals and Blood Flow Change with Channeling

Electrical signals emitted from the brain can be measured from the scalp. This measurement is called electroencephalography, or EEG. These signals have different frequencies, or cycles per second, depending on the state of the brain. People who perform well on channeling tasks in the laboratory and well-known or high-performing psychics have increased alpha brain wave frequency (Radin and Pierce 2015). Alpha waves are generally associated with a relaxed yet alert state. They are also seen in higher brain functions, like attention, perception, working memory (i.e., short-term memory), and mental representations of objects and events. Higher alpha brain waves are also found in most meditation studies (Cahn and Polich 2006; Lomas, Ivtzan, and Fu 2015) and transcendent states during meditation (Wahbeh, Sagher, et al. 2018).

In mediumship studies, the EEG signals were different when mediums engaged in various activities such as imagining things versus connecting with a deceased person (Delorme et al. 2013). Mediums also have differences in their brains when they give correct compared to incorrect answers about the deceased person (Delorme et al. 2018).

Trance channeler studies also found differences in brain waves and increases in noradrenaline, muscle tone, and heart rate during channeling sessions (Bastos et al. 2015, 2016; Hageman, Krippner, and Wickramasekera 2011). This general pattern reflects dissonance. For example, the trance channelers' muscles are tense, but their brain waves are relaxed.

I have watched trance channelers channel since I was ten years old—their whole body changes when they go into the channeling state, as do their mannerisms and their voice. Everything about them is different. If I closed my eyes, I would not know it was my mom or uncle or grandmother in front of me. These personal experiences drove me to do my own trance channeling study. We recorded body measures before, during, and after trance channeling (Wahbeh et al. 2019): brain waves, heart waves, breathing rates, skin electrical activity, and voice. We found voice differences but nothing else. We think this is because we had the channelers switch back and forth from channeling to not channeling every five minutes, which likely affected the results.

You live in Brazil and discover you have a tumor growing in your abdomen. You wait in line for hours for your local spiritual healer. They are a trance healer-medium who commonly performs surgery. It is your turn. You step up to the table and lie down for your "trance surgery." The surgery is done without anesthesia or sterilization procedures that you would typically expect in a hospital. You feel comfortable though. You know many people who have had surgeries from this healer without problems. The procedure begins. You feel relaxed and calm; in fact, it feels like you are almost asleep. Before you know it, the surgery is complete. You did not feel any pain. All you felt were some tugging sensations. You go back to the hospital the next week. The Western doctor confirms that the tumor is gone and is amazed.

Many Brazilian communities depend on or choose to go to the spiritual healers or trance healer-mediums for surgery procedures. One field study observed several thousand patients being treated by nine trance surgeons (Don and Moura 2000). The brain waves of the trance surgeons were different during trance states and showed increased arousal. Amazingly, so were the patients' brain waves. The patients' brain waves reflected a more relaxed brain and body, despite a lack of anesthesia!

Finally, another group of researchers looked at brain blood flow during automatic writing—where a spirit supposedly writes through the medium's hand (Peres et al. 2012). The blood flow in specific brain areas responsible for mental processes was lower in the trance state than in the ordinary writing state. This means that the channeler's brain was thinking more during the nontrance state. This was remarkable because the writing during trance was much more complicated than nontrance writing. You would expect that blood flow to parts of the brain that process cognition would be higher during complex writing. It was not.

Is the Pineal Gland a Channeling Organ?

Another research area proposes that the pineal gland and the compounds it creates are involved in channeling (Roney-Dougal 1989; Roney-Dougal and Vogl 1993; Bragazzi et al. 2018).

Called the "seat of the soul" by Descartes (Lokhorst 2018), the pineal gland is a small gland deep within the brain that produces the hormones melatonin and serotonin. These hormones affect our body's daily and seasonal cycles. The pineal's hormones are most active in the middle of the night. Interestingly, people do better on psi tasks at the height of pineal hormone activity (3:00 a.m.) versus other times of the day (Luke 2015).

The pineal gland is also the suspected production site within the body of dimethyltryptamine, or DMT. DMT is a powerful hallucinogen linked with channeling experiences (Luke 2012, 2015). People have been taking DMT as a drug for around twenty years. Because of this drug use, we have learned much about DMT and its effects.

However, we don't know much about the DMT that is produced within the body. If you do a search online, you'll see an assumed connection between the human pineal gland and DMT. But researchers haven't found DMT in the human pineal gland. Only one study found it in the pineal glands of rodents (Barker 2018).

That doesn't mean that the pineal gland and DMT are not involved in channeling. It just means that it remains a mystery. One study looked at DMT levels in mediums after a session. They found no DMT difference between mediums versus nonmediums (Bastos, Bastos, dos Santos, et al. 2018). This study is just the beginning. When people take DMT as a drug, you can see it in the urine for twenty-four hours, saliva for one to five days, and hair for ninety days. However, we are still unsure how natural DMT is processed in the body (Barker 2018).

The relationship between geomagnetic fields and channeling provides more convincing evidence for the pineal gland being involved in channeling in some way. The sun regularly discharges charged particles. These travel through space and come to Earth, where they change Earth's magnetic field. These geomagnetic changes affect our body's physiology, especially our cardiovascular system and mental health (Kiznys, Vencloviene, and Milvidaité 2020; Nishimura et al. 2020).

Geomagnetic fields also affect channeling phenomena. Overall, most studies show that receptive channeling, like mind-to-mind communication or seeing distant information, is more likely to occur on low geomagnetic activity days. Expressive channeling, like psychokinesis or seeing a ghost, happens on days of high geomagnetic activity (Ryan 2015). Maybe we see these effects because geomagnetic fields affect our bodies, rather than being directly involved in the reception or expression of some information or force (Ryan 2015). That is where the pineal gland comes in.

Our pineal gland is affected by geomagnetic activity. The pineal gland is unique because it can detect light (Vigh et al. 2002) and magnetism (Lerchl, Nonaka, and Reiter 1991). Other parts of our body have photoreceptors that detect light, including our eyes and skin. However, the pineal gland is nestled deep within our brain, in the exact center of our brain. Perhaps the geomagnetic activity acts on the pineal gland, which increases or decreases DMT levels, which then influences channeling experiences (Ryan 2015).

Sometimes it seems as if we have more questions than answers about the pineal gland, geomagnetic effects, and channeling. Still, we learn more clues about how they may be involved with each study. There is undoubtedly an allusion to the pineal gland being involved somehow through channeled material, which I will share later.

You have learned a few things about channeling from studies on neurotransmitters and hormones, electrical activity and blood flow, and the pineal gland and geomagnetic activity. You have read about the brain differences in channeling and nonchanneling states that show the channeling brain is usually in an alert but relaxed state, similar to meditation. This supports the idea that the brain is a receiver or antennae rather than a generator of channeled information. Of course, I have glossed over many details and nuances about these studies, and we need a lot more research to confirm this. In trance channeling, the body is conversely in an aroused state. Also, the pineal gland and DMT may be involved in channeling, but there is still a lot more research that needs to be done to confirm this as well.

Reflect on the various ways the channeling-body interface has been studied. Do you think using physiological correlates is a useful way to learn about how channeling works? What are your ideas about the body and how it relates to your channeling experiences?

Summarizing How Channeling Works

From all of these scientific studies, models, and theories, what can you say about how channeling works? Well, channeling is most likely not a force. Channeling transcends our conventional notions of time and space. Perhaps channeling works because we are all interconnected and part of an informational Universe. And your behaviors and choices, whether conscious or unconscious, co-create your reality of what you see around you. Your body is clearly affected by channeling. You can usually see changes in the body in a channeling versus nonchanneling state. The pineal gland and DMT may or may not be involved in some way. What we clearly do know is that we still don't know precisely how channeling works.

For those of you who have had channeling experience, you might "just know" how it works without knowing it mentally. It just is. It is an ineffable experience, meaning that it is challenging to put into words. On some level, it really doesn't matter how it works. You just know that it does. But that little girl sitting in front of the disassembled toy still wants to know. Thankfully, I have other ways of trying to understand how channeling works besides scientific inquiry. I can use channeling.

Learning How Channeling Works Through Channeling

I asked trance channelers to describe how channeling works during channeling (Anastasia et al. 2020; Wahbeh, Carpenter, and Radin 2018). I received quite interesting results. The overall message was that all humanity can channel. Multiple factors influence the type of channeling and information a person can access. One aspect is the person's willingness to channel. The person's spiritual awareness or maturity is another. The communicators made it clear that they didn't mean some people were better than or worse than others. People's spiritual development exists on a continuum, and some people are more ready than others to access channeled information. The third factor was the person's "frequency" and "energy structure," which is partly determined by their genetic makeup. One channeler said the following:

> Each channeler has their own general frequency and specific frequencies
> within their body (mental, emotional, physical—the organs, tissues, and
> so forth). Then energy packets get merged into the channeler's energy.
> This merging is why the same being in different channels appears different.
> It is a comingling of the channeler's and "being's" energy.

I found this point quite interesting because we've already noticed that some channeling experiences seem to run in families. Another factor is what the communicators called the "library of the mind." This referred to the channelers' education, vocabulary, languages spoken, and so forth. The library of the mind apparently influences how the communicator can communicate.

Despite my desire for one straightforward mechanism, they also shared that there is no one way that trance channeling works. Channeling takes many forms and is dependent on "frequency."

- Information can be downloaded as energy packets through the crown.

- The "being" can use the brain (i.e., use the verbal equipment to speak or extend itself to control the body).

- Some "beings" do not need to use the brain but can directly move the body through their own energy.

One "being" described their experience of communicating through the trance channeler:

My frequency is so high that I can move through you. You're made up of a bunch of particles, and there's more space in your body than there is matter. But then if I lower my frequencies, it makes [it] difficult for me to get into the empty spaces, and that gives me resistance or a grip when I come into the body. I'm trying to get the cells to vibrate at a higher frequency to give me more space, and I lower my frequency so that I can stay in the body. But I don't belong in it…[not] permanently.

These comments are fascinating and worthy of future study. Often the words "energy" and "frequency" are used by people experiencing channeling. The way these terms are being used are likely not the same as they are used in physics. We have yet to develop tools that can measure or see these "frequencies." We are working with multiple collaborators, including the Consciousness and Healing Initiative,[27] to discover how we can measure "energy" and "frequency."

Similar information came through another channeling session. I was working on this chapter as our shelter-in-place for the coronavirus pandemic happened. My mother's housing situation was too isolated and not ideal for a quarantine situation. She came to stay with us for a couple weeks. I shared my work on this chapter. She said I should ask my questions in a channeling session. We proceeded to do just that.

I asked the question after my mother went into her channeling state, "Can you explain how channeling works?"

The "beings" described that the way channeling happens depends on the person. They described a way of working with the body that works through the mental aspect of the brain. They also described the process of taking over a whole body, such that it would be more like a puppet. Channeling experiences like telepathy work differently from trance channeling. They were having difficulty finding the words in my mother's mind they wanted at a certain point. They couldn't communicate the points they wanted to make. I asked if they wanted to speak through me as an experiment. Because I had a different library of the mind than my mother due to my education and science background, perhaps they could communicate more clearly.

They agreed. I went into my meditative state and gave permission for the channeling to happen. I felt incredibly warm throughout my body. I felt a transcendent oneness that I always get when I trance channel. My boundaries dissolved, and I was filled with a sense of love, bliss, and peace. Miraculously, my mouth started moving. Words began to come out, but I had no idea what was going to be said. The part of me that was watching like an observer could hear what was being said. When I trance channel, I often get visuals about the information being communicated, but I don't know what will be said next. I can also interrupt the process at any point and regain control.

Here is a summary of what was said about how trance channeling works.[28] The pineal gland has a physical and energetic aspect. It receives information that it "translates" through the channeler to be spoken.[29] There is another type of trance channeling that is complete incorporation. In this, it goes through the pineal gland again. But this time, the "being" inhabits the channeler's energetic matrix. It fills the entire cells and vital force of the body. It does not remove the channeler's vital force but synchronizes with it. If the channeler gives permission, then it takes over.[30]

The pineal gland can receive light. Channeled information is sent through specific multidimensional light structures or constructs, and the pineal gland can read this information. It then gets translated into the energetic matrix of the body in cooperation with the DNA. DNA is like a being within the cells. It is an information warehouse but also an information manager.

Channeling experiences, like telepathy and other receptive psi, work differently. The information can be accessed consciously or unconsciously from one person to another. It also gets filtered through the pineal gland. The information packet (in the form of a light matrix) can go from one person to another. This can happen in a directed way. It also occurs unconsciously from people's thought-forms. Like the heart waves resonate out from the physical heart, thought waves similarly have a signature. The missing piece is that the information is multidimensional. The information already exists layer upon layer upon layer. It is accessed, and there can be a directionality to it. When somebody intends to have information accessed in a specific way, it has directionality in time and space. They went on to say:

> So, we will see if that answered your question in any way. We know that you would love to have a simple answer, but there is not a simple answer. Each aspect of what you are calling psi, or the noetic experience, is done differently. It is like an infinite number of characteristics that come together. There is the person who is accessing. There is the being who may be transmitting or the information that is being received. There is the content of that. There is the situation. All of these come into play in terms of how it happens. So, there is no one solution. There are multiple solutions. It is not a force per se. It is not force-like; it is informational. And yet that information can manifest in a force-like way. There are force-like outcomes that come from the information.

Incredibly, the information communicated in this session was similar to that received in our other studies. It is also noteworthy that some of what we see coming to light today about quantum entanglement, information theory, and our channeling experiments support what was said in my trance channeling session. We still have a long way to go, though, to understand in a scientific way how channeling works. What is clear is that there is no one answer. There are likely multiple ways in which channeling works. The process is individual and depends on many factors. Let's explore some of the factors that make channelers unique.

CHAPTER 6

What Do Channelers Have in Common?

In my family, channeling was commonplace. We were all able to tune in and access information and energy, and to channel. I wasn't sure if other families were the same. As a younger person, I thought everyone who channeled experienced it as I did.

I grew up beyond my younger self-centric world view. I realized that people experienced channeling in different ways. No, not everyone could feel the energy when they walked into a room. Or feel the emotions of others around them. Or see energy fields around people. Their channeling experiences were different from mine. I also noticed that some people did not have any abilities, or at least not any that they were aware of and were willing to share. I often wondered, *Are only certain people able to channel? Do those people have unique qualities that allow them to channel? Are they only able to do certain types of channeling? What makes channelers unique?*

In this chapter, I'll answer some of these questions, and we'll look at some of the many studies that focused on the characteristics of people who channel.

Channelers' Characteristics

Individual characteristics, like age, race, gender, religious affiliation, and psychological characteristics, have been studied in relation to channeling experiences. Most people in our channeling studies are older, well-educated, Caucasian women of higher economic status. They are also spiritual but not religious, empathetic, and highly sensitive. These are, of course, just some studies. Let's see what other studies note about the characteristics of a channeler.

Gender

In our studies, women usually report more and stronger experiences than men. Other studies have found similar results (Palmer and Braud 2002). This was especially true for precognition, extrasensory perception, mystical experiences, telepathy, and after-death communication in one study (Castro, Burrows, and Wooffitt 2014b). Women are also more likely to try different channeling types (Bader, Mencken, and Baker 2017). Women usually also have stronger beliefs in channeling (Irwin 2009), though not in all studies (Lindeman and Aarnio 2006). Most of these studies were done in the West. Results of studies in cultures where channeling is part of the spiritual tradition and the channeler's role is filled by a man were contrary to these Western results.

In general, women encompass more yin qualities. Yin qualities are receptive and open (Klimo 1998). Perhaps it is the feminine/yin principle of receptivity that makes channeling possible rather than gender. In our world today, the concept of gender has become more fluid. More and more people are embracing their masculine and feminine aspects, regardless of gender. Perhaps as this becomes more commonplace, there will not be such a gender difference in channeling survey studies in the West.

Age

The relationship between channeling and age is not as clear. One study found older people had more experiences, whereas another found younger people did.

Many people in our studies who had their first experience when they were younger have more experiences as adults. We saw that in about twelve hundred people who said they experienced mediumship (Wahbeh and Radin 2018), and in nine hundred scientists, engineers, channeling enthusiasts, and the general public in the United States (Wahbeh, Radin, et al. 2018). Others have seen this as well (Gilbert 2010). This is less true of trance channeling. First-time trance channeling usually happens later in life (Wahbeh and Butzer 2020; Wahbeh et al. 2019; Wahbeh, Carpenter, and Radin 2018). In countries where channeling is more integrated with the culture, trance channeling can happen earlier, but not usually when people are children (Bastos et al. 2016; Bastos, Bastos, Osório, et al. 2018).

Studies of children happen less often than adult studies. Mostly this is because of ethical and logistical issues around researching children. When asked, children do say they have channeling experiences (Wulff 2000, 409). Past-life research in children is also a large area of study. Children often report memories of a past life with vivid detail. Many of these facts have been checked and found to be true. The University of Virginia's Division of Perceptual Studies has had an ongoing research program on this for over fifty years.

Race

Our surveys were also mostly completed by Caucasians. One study found that people with Black or Asian/Pacific Islander heritage were less likely to report channeling experiences (Wahbeh, McDermott, and Sagher 2018). Others have found no differences in race for paranormal beliefs or experiences (Fox 1992; French and Stone 2013). Most studies, however, look at race differences within particular countries and are dependent on their social norms. Few studies look at channeling experiences across different cultures (Haraldsson 1985; Höllinger and Smith 2002). There are serious limitations in research looking at racial differences in channeling. No studies that I know of look at racial differences across countries. As far as we know, channeling is a global phenomenon.

Religion and Spirituality

In our studies, people who associated with the "spiritual but not religious" affiliation had more channeling experiences. Many respondents also had been raised Christian but endorsed "spiritual but not religious" as adults. This trend is also seen in large surveys in the United States (Hackett, Grim, and Kuriakose 2012; Lipka and Gecewicz, 2017). People with religious or spiritual values are more likely to have channeling experiences (Bouchard et al. 1999). As we saw in chapter 1, most religious and spiritual traditions worldwide have some form of channeling as part of their background or rituals.

Psychology

In chapter 3, you saw the relationship between mental health and channeling experiences. In general, people who have channeling experiences have higher dissociative and psychotic symptoms, although they don't usually reach clinical levels. Higher dissociative symptoms are also tied to gender because women tend to dissociate more than men (Klimo 1998). Perhaps some level of dissociation makes it easier to access transcendent states and extrasensory information. People with channeling experiences also have a greater chance of having a history of trauma or sexual abuse, which is also associated with dissociative symptoms (Klimo 1998; Sagher, Butzer, and Wahbeh 2019; Rabeyron and Loose 2015).

Extensive research has been done on paranormal belief and channeling experiences, as you learned about in chapter 4 (Rapoport, Leiby-Clark, and Czyzewicz 2018). People with greater beliefs have more channeling experiences and do better on tasks in the laboratory.

Numerous studies have looked at people's personality characteristics and channeling experiences. The most common personality test measures the big-five traits: openness, conscientiousness, extraversion, agreeableness, and neuroticism.[31] People who experience channeling also score higher on extraversion and openness to experience (Cardeña and Marcusson-Clavertz 2015; Wahbeh, Radin, et al. 2018; Roxburgh and Roe 2011). People who score high on extraversion (Honorton, Ferrari, and Bem 1998; Rattet and Bursik 2001) and openness to experience (Hitchman, Roe, and Sherwood 2012; Luke, Roe, and Davison 2008) do better on various laboratory tasks. Being open to experience and extroverted are the personality characteristics most related to channeling experiences.

The personality characteristic of neuroticism is not so clear (Cardeña and Marcusson-Clavertz 2015; Roe, Henderson, and Matthews 2008; Roxburgh and Roe 2011; Wahbeh, Radin, et al. 2018). People with high neuroticism scores are more likely to experience negative emotions, like anxiety, worry, and fear, and respond worse to stressors. Maybe people who are more concerned about the world around them are also more sensitive to it. That is, they may be more vigilant to other sources of information. Hypervigilance is a key symptom in stress disorders. It can be debilitating when severe. Perhaps some hypervigilance supports greater openness. Maybe low-level hypervigilance increases one's capacity to "tune in" to other extrasensory input.

Besides personality characteristics, certain states are favorable for channeling. One is called transliminality, or thin mental boundaries (Lange et al. 2000; Rabeyron and Loose 2015). Transliminality means that a person is hypersensitive to images, ideas, perceptions, and emotions from their unconscious or external environment (Lange et al. 2000; Thalbourne 2000). Others call this psychic permeability (Harrison and Singer 2013).

Another trait helpful for channeling is called sensory processing sensitivity. Sensory processing sensitivity refers to a sensitivity to stimuli, deep processing of information, and more emotional and physiological reactivity (Aron and Aron 1997). In our studies, people who channel reported higher sensory processing sensitivity levels than those who didn't. This may also be related to empathy, or relating to the emotions of others. People with channeling experiences can also score higher on empathy scales, which we and others have seen (Irwin 2017).

Along with a permeability of a person's awareness and sensitivity to the environment and other people, absorption is usually high in people who channel. *Absorption* refers to someone's inclination to become wholly absorbed in situations with their total attention. This complete attention fully engages their senses, imagination, and ideas (Tellegen and Atkinson 1974). For example, when you watch a TV show, do you get so involved in it that you forget what is around you? My cousin would always make fun of me when I watched shows as a child. She would try to talk to me, and I couldn't hear her. I was so engrossed in the show, it was as if I were there in the story. I had the same experience with reading books and watching movies. I was utterly engaged in the story and not aware of anything around me. I would often get disoriented after a movie was over and need some time to adjust back to the "real world." Usually, people with high absorption scores report more channeling experiences (Cardeña and Marcusson-Clavertz 2015; Wahbeh et al. 2019; Sagher, Butzer, and Wahbeh 2019; Hageman, Krippner, and Wickramasekera 2011).

In summary, there are some general trends for individual characteristics of people who have more channeling experiences or do better on tasks in the laboratory:

- female

- spiritual but not religious

- high channeling belief

- openness to experiences

- extroverted, empathetic

- highly sensitive

- thin mental boundaries

- high absorption

This doesn't mean that if you don't have these characteristics, that you can't channel. It just means that the studies done so far have noted these characteristics.

What about these characteristics do you think supports or could support channeling in you? Are any of these characteristics true for you? What are some of the limitations of studying the characteristics of channelers? What are some of the benefits?

Meditation Improves Channeling

On the other hand, meditation is one of the strongest predictors for channeling experiences or doing well on channeling tasks. Most meditation traditions talk about how advanced meditators have channeling experiences. The oldest descriptions are in the *Yoga Sutras*, in which about twenty-five channeling experiences, or *siddhis*, are presented. These revolve around three major categories: (1) exceptional mind control over the body, (2) the ability to "see" beyond time and space (clairvoyance, precognition, telepathy), and (3) having mental control over the physical world. Dean Radin (2013) gives a wonderful, easy-to-read review of the *siddhis* in his book *Supernormal*.

Some traditions invite the meditator to not make a big deal about these experiences. The meditator can apparently derail their spiritual progress by focusing on them. Apparently, they can be seductive, cause self-centeredness, or become distractions (Vivekananda 1893). Other traditions and advanced masters see them as essential milestones on the spiritual development path. Despite the dramatic increase in meditation research studies, few focus on channeling (Vieten et al. 2018).

Highly respected meditators have encouraged research on channeling despite this. Matthieu Ricard, a well-known Buddhist monk, was on a panel at a large meditation research conference. He was asked what he thought were the most important things the meditation research field should focus on next. He said reincarnation, past lives, and telepathy (Delorme 2013).

Regardless, meditating or being a meditator makes having a channeling experience more likely. We surveyed 1,120 meditators to see if they had channeling experiences during their meditation sessions. More than half said they had. They had experiences like clairvoyance and telepathy, alterations in time and space, and communications with nonphysical entities (Vieten et al. 2018). People who are in a meditative state are also likely do better on laboratory tasks (Roney-Dougal 2015).

What is it about meditators or meditating that makes channeling easier? Maybe it is because meditators train their attention. They can successfully concentrate and focus without letting outside stimuli bother them. Perhaps like the ganzfeld technique, clearing the mind makes accessing information not ordinarily available to our five senses easier.

Advanced meditators in Christian, Buddhist, Vedic, and mixed traditions also regularly experience transcendent states (Wahbeh, Sagher, et al. 2018). In all of these traditions, the transcendent states were described very similarly—as a blissful and joyful state of relaxed awareness outside of usual time and space. Perhaps regularly being in the transcendent states of timelessness and spacelessness allows access to a channeling state more easily.

Channeling Requires an Altered State of Consciousness

Studies do make it pretty clear that a person's state of awareness is essential for channeling. Usually, some form of an altered state of consciousness (ASC) supports channeling experiences. Hypnosis, ganzfeld, dreaming, drugs, meditation, and trance are all techniques used to support channeling (Cardeña and Marcusson-Clavertz 2015).

Some well-known trance channelers describe their experience during channeling as being asleep. My grandmother was like this. She would feel herself leaving her body and then "go to sleep." When she "returned" to her body, she had no recollection of what had transpired during the session.

Today we see variations in trance channelers' levels of consciousness during channeling. Some trance channelers are in deep trances. Others are totally aware of what is happening. They often describe their experience as observing the channeling while their body is being used. J. Z. Knight describes something similar when she channels Ramtha. On the other hand, Lee Carroll, who channels Kryon, explains that "he is conscious during the channeling, aware of all that Kryon says. He 'goes under' by using his own process of meditation and breathing, and in a few moments, he changes from Lee Carroll to Kryon. The entity speaks in Carroll's voice" (Guiley 2010, 83).

Channelers who are "asleep" are unaware of what is being communicated. They also do not remember anything afterward (Hughes 1991; Oohashi et al. 2002). Channelers who are "awake" may not remember anything later also. This is true of channelers I know. I have been in many channeling sessions over the last decade with my mother, who is "awake" when she channels. If I ask her about what she said a few days later, she can't remember. This is true even if the message is specifically for her and we talk about it directly after the session. This happens to me too. Even though I can hear what is being said when I am trance channeling, I can't remember what I said a few days later. Other trance channelers have also noted this (Wahbeh et al. 2019; Pederzoli et al. 2018).

People who experience other types of channeling, like feeling people's emotions, seeing distant places, or feeling the future, also have various awakeness states. It creates confusion when we define trance channeling with "trance" because that term can be so different based on who you are talking to.

We developed a unique way for channelers to tell us their awareness level during channeling. We asked people to rate their awareness during channeling on a scale of 0 to 100, with 0 being fully conscious and aware and 100 being fully unconscious and unaware. For our trance channeler studies, the average rating was around 47 (Wahbeh and Butzer 2020; Wahbeh et al. 2019). In our survey with various types of channelers, the rating was 35 (Wahbeh, Radin, et al. 2018). You'll notice that our trance channelers' average was pretty low (the range was 14–100).

While channeling experiences are all different, some altered state of consciousness is present. Trance channeling can still happen when someone is fully aware. These levels can also change over time. Someone who is "asleep" during trance channeling may find that they do not go fully asleep later in life while channeling. Regardless, surrender is a common theme. In most cases, the channelers feel a sense of surrender over to the purported being (Klimo 1998; Hastings 1991).

In what way have you found that meditative states affected your own channeling experiences? What have you noticed about your own consciousness level during meditation?

Channeling Runs in Families

I'm sure you've heard the idea that psychic abilities run in families. There are numerous anecdotes about this, but not many studies. One researcher looked at if "second sight" ran in families in multiple countries. Second sight is described as a natural prophetic ability of the mind. It happens spontaneously and is rarely controlled by the person with it.

Imagine "seeing" a funeral procession going by. You know whose funeral it is based on the people carrying the coffin, who know the person who passed away. The next day, you learn that the person had passed.

The second sight studies showed that people with second sight were more likely to report a blood relative with the ability (Cohn 1994). After doing extensive family pedigree interviews, the study also showed that inheritance was an autosomal dominant pattern (Cohn 1999). This means that if one of your parents has second sight, there is a 50 percent chance that you would have it. If both your parents had it, there is a 50 to 100 percent chance that you would have it.

Most people with various channeling abilities said that channeling runs in their family (58 to 70 percent) (Wahbeh, McDermott, and Sagher 2018; Wahbeh, Radin, et al. 2018). Those who did also had more potent and more frequent experiences. People with rare experiences, such as pyrokinesis or controlling fire, psychic surgery, psychokinesis, and trance channeling, said they had family members with the same abilities. For example, people who said they could generate or control fire with their mind were four times as likely to say that they had family members who could channel. People who experienced geomancy, or the ability to tune in to the energy of places and of the land, such as ley lines, were six times more likely to report a family member with the same ability.

But these are all self-report surveys. What about genetics or family tree studies? We wanted to know if genetics had anything to do with channeling skills, so we screened over three thousand people and narrowed it down to thirteen high-performing psychics. They went through multiple levels of tests and interviews. We wanted to include motivated, psychologically well-grounded people with testable psychic abilities.

It just so happened that all the psychics were older women. We then found controls who did not have any psychic abilities or family members with those abilities. Because we were looking at genetics, the controls' demographic characteristics of age, gender, and race had to match our psychics' demographics so that any differences we saw between the two groups were not a result of those aspects. For example, we had to find controls who were older women to match the older age and gender of the psychics. It took us a much longer time to find the controls. Apparently, it is challenging to find older women with no psychic abilities.

We finally collected saliva from all the participants to extract the DNA and decoded all their genes. We compared the gene sequences of the psychics to the controls. Much to our surprise, we found one section of the noncoding DNA that was conserved, or wild-type, in all the psychics but was variable in the controls. Wild-type means that the DNA sequence was the original version and was not mutated. That it was in a noncoding region of the DNA means that it was in a part that does not code for a protein. Instead, it likely acts to regulate the activity levels of its neighboring gene. The gene next to it is highly expressed in the brain. This supports the notion that this conserved region could influence gene activity related to psychic abilities (Wahbeh, Radin, et al. 2021).

Yes, channeling does run in families, especially for more rare channeling experiences. We are just beginning to understand what this possibly means. Everyone was so excited about the Human Genome Project, but the results were disappointing because our DNA's hard code didn't tell scientists as much as they thought it would. Epigenetics, or how genes are turned up or down, is turning out to be more exciting and significant. Likely this will be true for channeling as well. The results will probably not be black-and-white but shades of gray reflecting our individual variation.

Anyone Can Learn Channeling

I don't think psychic ability is hardwired. I believe anyone can learn to do it to a certain extent. Do you want to learn how to trance channel, or remote view, or bend spoons, or increase your telepathic powers? There are numerous books, videos, and classes at your fingertips to try. Do these actually work? Can anyone learn how to channel? Here are a few cases in psychokinesis, remote viewing, and trance channeling where I know it is possible for just about anyone to learn, at least at some level.

Learning Psychokinesis

I met Sean McNamara at IONS. Sean is a meditation teacher and consciousness exploration guide. His mission is to "provide people with the tools and techniques for exploring their consciousness, their spirituality, and reality, without dogma or religious overlay. This is about self-empowerment via direct experience" (McNamara 2019a).

Sean offered to teach our staff how to move objects with their minds. He created a simple setup to help people learn this. There is a cork with a pin in it. On top of the pin is a small piece of foil paper. The cork, pin, and foil paper are all sitting inside a glass jar. The trainee then relaxes completely using a special breathing technique. They direct an open and diffuse gaze on the foil paper. That's it. You just gaze at the foil paper while you are entirely relaxed with the goal of making it move. The glass jar prevents any air movement from affecting the foil.

I had the best results when I mentally imagined the foil already moving. The foil would then move. I also played with having the foil move one way and then the other with my directed intention. Sean said that he can teach anyone to move the foil with their mind if they believe they can do it. He said he has only had one person over his many years of training people who could not do it (McNamara 2019b).

Learning Remote Viewing

People can also get trained to remote view. Many organizations support remote viewing education and research, like the International Remote Viewing Association and Applied Precognition Project. Many experts think that anyone can learn and that training and practice improve people's ability. For example, the US Central Intelligence Agency document describes a remote viewing training procedure for soldiers who had never done it before (Hubbard and Langford 1986). Famous remote viewer Ingo Swann wrote a book for people to unlock their natural extrasensory perception, including remote viewing (Swann 2018).

Learning Trance Channeling

Because of my family's history and what I heard from other families, I used to think that only certain people could trance channel, that perhaps it was a genetic trait. My experience with hypno-channeling changed my mind.

I shared in the introduction that I was able to learn trance channeling through hypnosis. I grew up having other types of channeling experiences. I watched trance channeling myself but never tried it. My colleague Dr. Patrizio Tressoldi, a professor at the Università di Padova in Italy, shared a hypnosis protocol used to teach trance channeling. In the protocol, people first learn how to have an out-of-body experience (Facco et al. 2019). Then they learn how to trance channel. None of the people had ever experienced channeling before. Dr. Tressoldi and his team have had excellent results with hours of channeled sessions (Pederzoli et al. 2018).

Lubna Kharusi of Dira International in Oman has seen similar results. Kharusi and her colleague came to IONS for a brain wave study. We saw changes in her and another channeler's brain waves when they were channeling. Dira is an acronym for Kharusi's method: divine intuitive receptive awareness. Dira International believes "that being a channel of Source energy is an integral part of human capacity, but yet through conditioning and mental constructs, we have prevented ourselves from accessing this natural state of connection, limiting ourselves, because of the reinforced beliefs of socio-historical constructs of what people interpret and believe to be possible" (Kharusi 2020).

Kharusi uses hypnosis, meditation, and other tools to teach trance channeling in week-long workshops. She feels that anyone can learn how to trance channel. She says the only requirement is that they believe it is possible and are willing to try (Kharusi 2019).

What are your thoughts on whether channeling can be learned or is genetically determined? How have training and family affected your own channeling experiences?

We All Have the Capacity to Channel

These three examples show that you too can learn to channel even if you have no experience. I now believe that we are all born with the *capacity* to channel at some level based on my personal experience, my and other research studies, training program reports, and people's stories, and that channeling is part of our fundamental human nature.

I also believe that people are born with different abilities for different channeling types. For example, suppose one person took psychokinesis, remote viewing, and trance channeling classes. In that case, they may do really well at remote viewing and okay at the other two. Just like other abilities, people's abilities are on a standard bell curve. You can compare these abilities to sports or music. Some people are better at sports, while others are better musicians. The same is true with channeling.

For example, some channelers are more visual. They "see" information and energy that they wouldn't typically have access to, like auras around people, spirits, and energy moving. Others might be more auditory, where they "hear" information, like others' thoughts or their guides' guidance. Someone else might be kinesthetic, where they feel information and energy in their body. They get goosebumps when they make the right choice, or their knee hurts when their spouse's knee hurts. We'll talk more about the different ways people experience their channeling in chapter 8.

Just like taking thousands of basketball shots can improve your basketball skills, so too can practice improve your channeling. Through practice, you can increase your *skill* for specific channeling types. You may have an easier time learning some channeling types than others because of your *abilities*, just like everyone is not a professional basketball player. You can always practice to get better, but you will always do better at some channeling types than others based on your innate abilities.[32]

Despite differences in abilities and skills, everyone has the capacity to access the "force" in some way.

CHAPTER 7

Where Is the Information Coming From?

Many people express curiosity and sometimes even concern about where the information they receive comes from. This is especially true for mediumship and channeling experiences. Is the source your unconscious or higher self? Is it some larger universal field? Is it nonphysical beings that you can't experience with your five senses but can *somehow* experience through channeling? Maybe the source is a bit of all of these.

The short answer is that we don't definitively know what the source of channeling is. Many theories and evidence supporting different sources exist. Despite this, we can't confirm the source is one thing or another once and for all. In this chapter, you will explore different ideas about the source of channeling. You can then decide what you think for yourself. Let's start with a few channeling-experience examples from trance channeling to give you a sense of the type of information that comes through.

Channeled Creativity

Researchers and field experts of art, music, and literature have spent much time and resources attempting to validate the source of channeled creative works. While some cases are more convincing than others, there is no definitive answer as to whether the material came from some part of the channeler themselves, psychic channeling abilities, or deceased artists. In most cases, the talent level, piece complexity, speed of creation, and how the material arrives fully formed exceed the channeler's usual abilities.

For example, José Andrade grew up in poor conditions in Brazil and only finished elementary school. His mediumship developed in adulthood in a Spiritist/Kardecist temple.[33] José prepared himself to channel with prayer. He then put his hands into paint and onto a canvas. He proceeded to produce landscapes, still lifes, and portraits, often all at the same time. He worked very quickly. Each painting took no more than ten minutes. José would sign each painting with a different artist's name, such as Monet, Cézanne, van Gogh, Picasso, da Vinci, and Degas (Hageman, Krippner, and Wickramasekera 2011; Maraldi et al. 2014, 286).

Luiz Antônio Gasparetto was also a Brazilian medium. He produced numerous paintings he believed came from famous deceased artists including Degas, Renoir, Toulouse-Lautrec, Manet, and many others. Luiz began automatic writing and drawing at thirteen years old. He used both hands at the same time and on different parts of the painting. Sometimes he even painted with his feet! The average time for him to complete a painting was ten to twenty minutes. Some were completed in as little as thirty seconds (Maraldi and Fernandes 2020; Hastings 1991, 167; Braude 2003, 168–69).

Rosemary Brown is another example of a medium who channeled artistic talent far beyond what we would expect from her background. Rosemary was a British medium who first channeled as a child. Apparently, Liszt told her when she was seven years old, he would return later in her life to give her music. As an adult, Rosemary created mostly piano pieces supposedly from Liszt, Chopin, Schumann, Schubert, and other deceased composers (Hastings 1991, 165; Braude 2003, 166–168).

Srinivasa Ramanujan was another example. He was an outstanding mathematical theorist in the early 1900s. He believed he channeled his formulas from the Indian goddess Namagiri and the Indian deity of language, song, and logic, Saraswati (Hastings 1991, 18).

One final example is perhaps the most remarkable. Pearl Curran was an American housewife who was born in 1883 and lived in the Midwest. Pearl's friend encouraged her to play the Ouija board with her. After the first year, they received a very clear message from a personality called Patience Worth. This began a life-long journey of channeling over forty-three hundred single-spaced pages of literary material[34] (Braude 2003, 133–34). Pearl/Patience's work is astonishing. Pearl/Patience would start channeling a work, stop in the middle, and then pick it up sometimes much later in the exact spot she had stopped. Also, the pieces seemed to be channeled fully formed with no editing needed.[35]

Where do you think this creativity comes from? Are goddesses and deceased paint-
ers or composers' really the sources of these channeled works? If you channel big
ideas, artwork, or stories, what do you believe the source of the channeled informa-
tion or energy is?

Many models attempt to explain the source of channeled material. Let's explore some of the major ones.

Source Model 1: The Unconscious Mind

One source ascribed to channeled information is the channeler's unconscious mind. The unconscious mind can be understood as the information you perceive but are not consciously aware of. This includes processes like judgments, decisions, and reasoning that happen without you knowing it.

Dr. Sigmund Freud highlighted the unconscious mind with his psychological theories and therapeutic methods. Freud thought the unconscious mind was the primary motivator of your daily actions, even though you don't know what is in it. Dr. Roberto Assagioli, a prominent psychologist, developed a model of the mind that includes a lower, middle, and higher unconscious (Assagioli 1965). Channeling relates most to the higher unconscious mind, which Assagioli suggests has the noble qualities of "intuition, inspiration, creativity, ethical impulses, altruism, humanitarian, and heroic impulses" (Hastings 1991, 180).

Perhaps channelers like Andrade and Gasparetto had artistic talents buried in their unconscious mind, despite their limited background. When channeling, we may give ourselves permission to have that talent rise to the surface and express itself. Besides talent, the unconscious mind could generate noble ways of being outside our usual way of being.

Channeling may allow your unconscious mind to find a way of expression. If you can't usually express yourself fully, channeling may let you do so. Imagine a woman working at home as a mother of five children. Her culture expects her to be quiet, raise the children, and have little power over her situation. That culture also has an organized social structure that considers channelers valuable, meaningful, and powerful in society. If the woman became a channeler, that role would allow her to express herself in ways that she usually could not. The unconscious mind could manifest channeling as a way for her to express herself more fully.

If the unconscious mind is the source of channeled material, then we must accept these three things:

Our mind creates remarkable experiences. This was definitely true for Pearl/Patience, who would produce entire completed literary works of exceptionally high quality. The speed in which Andrade and Gasparetto channeled their paintings and the variety of styles of their work are similarly quite extraordinary.

Our unconscious mind can access information or talent that is not ordinarily available to us. Many channelers bring forth information that is far beyond their typical education or talent level. For example, Pearl/Patience's literary accomplishments were far beyond her conscious capacity.

The unconscious mind can quickly generate various well-developed personalities with particular characteristics. Some channelers can channel multiple different personalities, one after the other, without a break. They can also give precise and detailed information about deceased people's lives.

The unconscious mind could very well be the source of channeling material by allowing you to somehow access remarkable information and talent far beyond your usual abilities.

Source Model 2: Our Transpersonal Selves

Aspects of your consciousness that go beyond the limits of your personal identity or "I" are called the transpersonal mind. Another theory is that your transpersonal selves are the source of channeled information. Some believe that what you know and experience as your "self" in your daily life is only one small part of your whole self.

Transpersonal aspects of your mind are intuitive, are creative, have purpose and meaning, and embody higher values (Hastings 1991, 180). Transpersonal experiences are inspirational or peak experiences where the Universe is perceived as harmonious and unifying and may directly contact what is described as God's consciousness or the Divine. They can occur spontaneously with meditation, prayer, natural beauty, sexuality, and other experiences (Hastings 1991, 193).

The higher self is one transpersonal aspect of the mind (Assagioli 1965). It is unconditionally loving. It supports you in aspiring to higher values, such as love, kindness, compassion, healthy emotions, thoughts and behaviors, and spiritual development (Hastings 1991, 180). The higher self is still a part of you, but it is a part of you that you may not be aware of. You can also experience the higher self as a separate entity within you. According to this model of the mind, everyone has a higher self.

Channeled material does support this notion. In one of our studies, one "being" shared that trance channelers are channeling an aspect of themselves, or their higher self. The incorporated "beings" are multidimensional aspects of the channeler themselves. They said:

> The channeler and the channeled being are aspects of each other. It is an illusion that we are separate. Understand at this time that humans still like the voice from above to convey messages. At some point, there will be no channeling anymore as you become the higher dimensional beings that you are channeling.

The collective unconscious is another transpersonal concept that may be the source of channeling. The collective unconscious is part of the unconscious mind that comes from our ancestry and all humans' experience. It is not your individual unconscious, but the unconscious aspects of all humanity (Sørensen 2016).

Channeled personalities. Parapsychologists have thought deeply about the source of mediumistic communication. Four sources of channeled personalities have been proposed: psi, superpsi, psychic reservoir, and survival. Let's assume that the usual and unusual suspects, like fraud and mental illness, have been ruled out.[36] Here is a typical case that I'll use as an example as we explore these four sources.

> Amy's father has just died. Danny had dementia and multiple strokes. He had been suffering for ten years with an increasing inability to function and communicate. Amy and her family were the primary caregivers for Danny in their home. There were many years before he passed that she was unable to communicate with him. Amy believed in life after death

*and had heard about mediums. She wanted to see if she could connect
with her dad's spirit, so she made an appointment with a recommended
medium. Before and at the meeting, Amy didn't tell the medium anything
about her father. She said she just wanted to connect with a loved one
who had recently passed on.*

*Amy was amazed. The medium gave her mostly accurate details
about her father's life and personality. The medium also shared that her
dad had met his wife (Amy's mother) and his mother (Amy's
grandmother), who had already passed. He expressed deep love and
gratitude to Amy and her family for caring for him in his later years. He
also shared that he was joyful and no longer in pain. He wished her to be
happy and satisfied in her own life and move on from the heaviness that
his illness caused their family. Amy left the session with a sense of relief
and joy. She knew she would still miss her father and feel sadness and
grief. She also felt like she could now let go and move on with her life.*

Source Model 3: Psi

In the psi model, the medium is telepathically picking up the information
from Amy's mind. Because Amy, who is referred to as the "sitter," is in front of
the medium, the medium can retrieve information from her. This is also
sometimes called "living-agent psi" because the medium is communicating
mind-to-mind with a living person, or Amy in this case (Beischel and Rock
2009). This seems like a reasonable theory, and you saw numerous studies
about it in chapter 4.

Source Model 4: Superpsi

Superpsi is like psi on steroids. In the superpsi model, the medium gets information from the sitter through telepathy. They would also use multiple other
channeling types, such as clairvoyance, precognition, or telepathy, to get
information.

In Amy's example, imagine that Amy could not find an essential legal
document her father placed somewhere. She then asked her "dad" through
the medium where the form was. Amy did not know where it was, so the

medium could not get its location through telepathy with Amy. The medium could, however, use clairvoyance to "view" its location. Perhaps, Danny told his lawyer where the document was without Amy knowing it. The medium could telepathically receive that information from the lawyer's mind. Some of the verified information mediums receive is quite complicated. It seems unlikely that mediums could receive multiple streams of complex information in this way and so quickly. It would also take an incredibly talented person to do this. Talent at this level is not seen in laboratory settings.

Some say that superpsi works like a magic wand. The information the medium receives is guided by their wish or desire. It is described as if the medium waves a magic wand, and the information they need to know is there for them (Braude 2003, 10–11). In this way, the medium does not intentionally direct their abilities to Amy's mind, the lawyer's mind, or remote viewing the document. The medium just has a need to know the information. Then, it appears through multiple avenues without them having to orchestrate how they get that knowledge. The information they need just appears. This magic wand idea is very similar to what you saw with the goal-directed effects in chapter 4. The person has a goal to make a red light increase. And it does, regardless of the steps it requires for the red light to actually increase. The medium has the goal to receive the information, and the Universe provides it without the medium knowing all the steps that allowed them to receive that information.

Source Model 5: Psychic Reservoir

Another model for where information comes from in mediumistic sessions is called a psychic reservoir. A psychic reservoir means that all the information in the Universe from all time is stored somewhere that mediums can access (Rock, Beischel, and Cott 2009; Fontana 2005). You may have heard of the term Akashic record. The Akashic record is believed to be the repository of every thought, word, and deed of every living being, in all time, past, present, and future. Interestingly, the modern promotion of the Akashic record came from Madame Helena Petrovna Blavatsky. She claimed to channel the information from Master Koot Hoomi, a teacher she met during her travels in India (Hastings 1991, 79). With the psychic reservoir model, the medium would access a psychic reservoir to receive information about Amy's dad.

Source Model 6: Survival After Death

Psi, superpsi, and psychic reservoir, if true, are quite remarkable. If they were proven and accepted, they would dramatically change how we view the world. However, mediums and sitters believe they are actually connecting with the deceased person themselves. They believe the person's consciousness has survived.

The survival model supposes that your consciousness in some form continues after your body dies (Beischel, Mosher, and Boccuzzi 2017). Studies have asked mediums to tell the difference between information they received from a deceased person versus psychic abilities. Mediums said they could do so and described the differences between these two experiences (Rock, Beischel, and Cott 2009; Beischel, Mosher, and Boccuzzi 2017).

Much of the academic literature on survival is focused on verifying the information mediums receive from the deceased person. The verification of the information is focused on facts about a person's life.

For example, let's imagine a researcher is reviewing a trance channeling session done for Amir, where he communicated with his grandmother Leila. His grandmother passed forty years ago. Amir wonders if it was really his grandmother because her personality seemed different. She spoke differently and didn't have the mannerisms he remembered about his grandmother. The medium provided Amir with about twenty facts that a researcher could verify. Amir and the researcher could only confirm fifteen of the points Leila provided. Amir and the researcher could then decide that it wasn't really Leila because it didn't seem like her, and she didn't get all the facts right from the questions asked about her worldly life.

There are assumptions inherent in this decision. They assume that Leila will retain her memories, facts, and specific details of her worldly life in the afterlife, and that Leila's personality will stay the same forty years after leaving her physical body. They also accept that she would remember everything that happened in her earthly life. They even suppose that Leila would be available to communicate through the medium at the time of the session (i.e., she was not busy).

Let's assume for a moment that our consciousness does survive our physical body's death. There is so much that we don't know about what that afterlife may look like. How can we make all these assumptions of how a deceased person would be or remember and decide that survival is not real based on that? While I might not say that our personality and memories survive precisely as they were in life, strong evidence exists that something persists. Exploring all the evidence for postmortem survival is beyond this book's scope. There are excellent resources available for you to go more deeply into this topic.[37]

Where do mediums receive their information from? If you channel personalities, what do you think is the source?

The unconscious mind, transpersonal selves, psi, superpsi, survival—can we choose a model that best represents the source of channeling? I don't think we can. Each case has different characteristics that fit some models better than others. All these models have supporting evidence, some more than others.

Personally, I find it hard to believe that the unconscious mind could generate all trance channeling phenomena. Perhaps in some situations, the source could be the unconscious mind where the person has access in the background or education on the material they are channeling. Some aspects of the theory that the transpersonal self is the source of channeled material are more plausible.

Let's see what people who channel think the source of their channeling is.

What Do Channelers Think the Source Is?

While we may never definitively know the true source of channeled information, we can certainly learn more about what people *think* the source is. People's understanding of the source is valuable, regardless of whether we can "prove" what it is. The study of people's experiences is called phenomenology. So, what do people experience as the source of the information or energy they receive?

There are common categories that people say are the sources of channeling. These include the person's higher self, God/gods/deities, the universal mind and the collective unconscious, ascended masters, spirits of deceased humans, earthbound spirits, group beings, and nonhumans (angels, devas, elementals, plants and animals, extraterrestrials) (Klimo 1998, 193–210;

Hastings 1991, 199). Some of these categories may be unfamiliar to you. Here are descriptions for some of the more unique ones.

- Ascended masters are believed to be a community of beings who were once humans, evolved on Earth, and reached a point where they were completely balanced and so did not return to Earth for another physical life.

- Group beings are believed to be a coherent bundle of still-individual or once-individual purported "beings" who communicate from a single integrated source.

- Earthbound spirits are believed to be deceased humans who have not transitioned to the light and stay stuck close to Earth. Apparently, this phenomenon typically happens when the individual has unresolved issues on Earth, died suddenly and unexpectedly, or was fearful of what would happen to them after death (i.e., annihilation).

- Elementals are believed to be conscious beings and guardians associated with the natural world like air, wind, fire, earth, trees, rivers, and so forth. Some have used names like fairies, pixies, or sprites.

We did two surveys asking people what they thought the source of their channeling was. They could choose as many sources as they wanted. One survey was with people who had various types of channeling experiences (mixed group). More than half of the participants chose their higher self (56 percent) as the source. The universal mind (50 percent), the collective unconscious (47 percent), and gods and/or God (43 percent) were the next most commonly chosen. Many people were not sure (44 percent). The remaining sources checked were deceased human beings (37 percent), angels (33 percent), Jesus Christ (24 percent), plants or animals (22 percent), other ascended masters (20 percent), group beings (16 percent), earthbound spirits (13 percent), elementals (9 percent), extraterrestrials (9 percent), and devas (6 percent) (Wahbeh, Radin, et al. 2018).

In a trance channelers survey, fewer were unsure of the source (25 percent). Like the mixed group survey, higher self (65 percent) was the most chosen source, followed by group beings (61 percent). More than half chose deceased humans as the source (56 percent). These categories were higher in the trance channelers: universal mind (51 percent), ascended masters (42 percent), earthbound spirits (32 percent), extraterrestrials (36 percent), plants or animals (26 percent), elementals (24 percent), and devas (15 percent). The following categories were lower in the trance channelers: the collective unconscious (44 percent), gods and/or God (26 percent), Jesus Christ (22 percent), and angels (3 percent) (Wahbeh and Butzer 2020).

The similarities and differences between these two studies are fascinating. In both studies, the higher self was the most commonly chosen source of channeling. Deceased human beings, the universal mind, and the collective unconscious were also present in both studies' top five. God and/or gods were chosen by 43 percent of the mixed group but only 26 percent in the trance channelers. Group beings were noted by 61 percent of the trance channelers, but only 16 percent of the mixed channeling group. The other more unusual answers, like extraterrestrials, elementals, and devas, were noted more often in the trance channeling group. Another interesting point is that most people chose more than one source, 75 percent in the mixed group and 85 percent in the trance channelers.

We did another study with five trance channelers where there were different sources. I was surprised by the incredible variety of supposed nonphysical beings that communicated through the five trance channelers at our focus group. Over three days, there were twenty-one different beings:

- Archangels (archangel Michael, Gabriel, and one unnamed);

- Ascended masters (Heyahwatha, Kathumi, Maitreya, Mother Mary, Mary Magdalene, Vovó Anamalia, Yeshua);

- Members of the deva kingdom;

- Extraterrestrials representing seven different star systems (Telos, Pleiadian, Arcturian, Sirian, Orion, Cygnus, Lyra);

- Two group beings (Galactic Beings of Light and Guardians of the Divine Feminine); and

- One earthbound spirit.

The ease with which the channelers moved from one being to another was incredible. The shift in their mannerisms, tone, vocabulary, and content with each new supposed being was astonishing.

Well-known trance channelers primarily channel one being (e.g., Esther Hicks and Abraham, Jane Roberts and Seth). In our trance channeler focus group, the most common channeling type was the traditional experience of one person channeling one being. However, not all trance channelers report channeling only one supposed source. There were also times where multiple channelers (up to four) channeled different beings simultaneously. In these cases, Ava would channel being A, Leora would channel being B, and Melissa would channel being C. In that channeling state, the beings A, B, and C would have a conversation with each other and the other people in the focus group.

Another time, multiple channelers channeled the same being right after each other. Ava would channel being D. Then, being D would say, "I'm going to move to Melissa now." After a minute, Melissa would then begin speaking as being D, continuing the line of conversation being D was on before the channeler switch. Being D then moved to Leora, repeating the process (Wahbeh, Carpenter, and Radin 2018). A fascinating process to observe.

Another unique aspect of this study was that we had our special RNG device in the corner of the room where the channelings were happening. The device is called a quantum noise generator (QNG) because it uses quantum-based noise (rather than 0s and 1s). It had thirty-two independent channels and emitted entirely random noise.

We then did two analyses. One looked at the relationship between the thirty-two different QNG channels (distortions in space). The other looked at the relationship of the data within each channel (distortions in time). We compared the channeling and nonchanneling periods. There was a difference! The data during channeling periods actually was less random than the nonchanneling periods.

These results are exciting for a few reasons. Personally, I have always "felt" a change in the environment when channeling happens. It has felt like there is electricity in the air, somewhat like it feels before a big lightning storm. Having the QNG data show that something was different in the environment validated what I was personally feeling. Why would the QNG data be different during channeling unless something really was different in the background? If the trance channelers were making up the personalities, I can't imagine why the data would be different. A follow-up study could have actors pretend to trance channel and see if the QNG results show any changes.

Anyway, I know this was just one small study, but it gives us some preliminary results we can build on with other studies. I can't "prove" that the beings in this study were who they said they were or where they were from. I can say that something was definitely happening during channeling that we wouldn't usually see.

Based on what people say the source of channeling is, there is no one source. So, what if that was true? What if the channeling source is actually multiple different sources depending on the channeler, the channeling type (mediumship, trance channeling, precognition, telepathy, etc.), and the situation? Mediums have reported that they connect to the deceased's spirit *and* use psychic experiences, and that they can tell the difference between the two (Beischel, Mosher, and Boccuzzi 2017; Rock, Beischel, and Cott 2009). Mediums also report that nonphysical beings support their sessions and can be the information source (Beischel, Mosher, and Boccuzzi 2017; Rock, Beischel, and Cott 2009). This is also true for other channeling types, such as energy medicine (Wahbeh, Niebauer, et al. 2020).

This concept of multiple sources may seem like common sense considering the different channeling types people can experience. Just like we saw with my search for the "how channeling works" holy grail, there is no holy grail for the channeling source. But is there?

The Larger We as the Source

You've learned about the various models of channeled sources people have proposed. You've also seen what people think the sources are, including multidimensional and nonphysical beings. However, perhaps all of these models are parts of a larger, more comprehensive model: "We are all one." This theme is repeated over and over again in the channeled material we have collected. All humanity and everything in the Universe are part of the same all-encompassing whole. If that is true, then whether the channeling source is your unconscious mind or your higher self or a nonphysical being, from a broader perspective, the source would ultimately be the same. True, the source may not be your personal self that you identify with every day. Yet, these other sources are still intrinsically linked to you.

One communicator expressed the oneness concept very understandably: everything is one and has consciousness. You can think of our universal oneness as being similar to the electromagnetic spectrum. You can view the electromagnetic spectrum as one thing, one consciousness. You can also view the electromagnetic spectrum as being many individual things. It is made up of all its different frequencies. Red, orange, yellow, green, blue, indigo, and violet all have their own unique graded frequencies. So do gamma waves and radio waves. Each of these frequencies is unique and has its own characteristics. And yet, it is also part of the one whole electromagnetic spectrum. So, you can think of yourself as one frequency on the universal spectrum—unique and individual and yet part of a larger whole.

This is not a new concept and is repeated in many spiritual traditions worldwide. Pantheism encompasses this idea. Pantheists believe that the Cosmos is the same thing as divinity or God. And that everything within the Cosmos is part of that whole. Also, there is nothing that exists that is outside of the whole. Ancient spiritual traditions like Hinduism, Kabbalistic Judaism, Celtic spirituality, and Sufi mysticism include pantheistic ideas (Mander 2020). You also see these ideas in modern popular media, such as:

- the Force in *Star Wars;*

- the tree of life and "flow of energy" that inhabits everything in *Avatar;* or

- the circle of life, encompassing unity and interconnection of all things, in *Lion King.*

As you've briefly seen in chapter 5, recent physics and cosmology discoveries support the idea of oneness. Using evidence from cosmological and physics studies, Dr. Currivan built a case that strongly supports that everything is interconnected and part of a whole. Also, the primary substance of that whole is information.

Dr. Currivan concludes that what I am calling channeling is possible in an informational view of the Cosmos. Channeling reflects the nonlocal aspects of our Universe. Channeling experiences give real-world examples showing that all parts of our world are informationally entangled, and it gives the ability know information from beyond time and space (Currivan 2017, 200).

Does the Source Matter?

Many researchers, especially from anthropology, say that the source is not essential (Luke 2014, 230; Gilbert 2014; Emmons 2014; Hunter 2014). Sociologist Hannah Gilbert says, "My interests were not concerned with whether or not mediums could scientifically prove that they were in contact with a real, interactive spirit world, but rather treated the spirit world as something *socially* real and meaningful" (Gilbert 2010, 63). Even if we can't know whether the information source is verifiably true or not, it is real and meaningful.

Your experience of channeling and the meaning it has in your life is most important. You can look at the material's meaningfulness and usefulness separately from whether you can verify it or its source. You can explore the content on its own and judge based on its own merit regardless of who created it. Psychologist and faculty member of Sofia University, James Fadiman explains, "The quality of the information is independent of the source" (Klimo 1998, 175).

Judith Skutch, a channeled material publisher, commented that similar messages from different channelers make the material more accessible to everyone. She said, "It doesn't matter what name one gives to the source" (Klimo 1998, 175). I have observed many channeling sessions where someone will invariably ask the communicator, "What is your name?" The answer to this question is usually something like, "Why are humans so preoccupied with names?" The communicators stress that the message itself rather than the message's source is most important in supporting humans individually and collectively. Psychologist Charles Tart said, "I don't count the content per se as evidence of independent existence. In this sense, you take something like *A Course in Miracles*. I find the content very inspiring and stimulating, but almost totally irrelevant to the question: Did this come from an independently existing disembodied entity? The fact that the content is inspiring and useful has almost nothing to do with the ontological status of the entity" (Klimo 1998, 175).

Not only do individuals find meaning in channeling experiences, but societies also do as well. Many cultures worldwide have structures that encompass channeling (e.g., Umbanda, Candomblé, and Kardecist Spiritism in Brazil). Channeling plays a vital role in these societies. Rather than dismissing channeling because we can't prove the source, why not study the experiences without being concerned about the source? Much can be learned about human consciousness and its capacities in this way.

What do you feel is the source(s) of your channeling? How does your perception of the source influence your relationship with your channeling? Do you think the source of channeling matters, and if so, why?

Channeling can bring significant meaning and insight into your life, even without verifying the source. It doesn't matter whether the source is our unconscious mind, higher self, a nonphysical being, or something else entirely. Likely, when we can "prove" such things, the source will be a combination of sources, depending on channeling type. What is more important, I feel, is to learn as much as we can about channeling from the meaning and importance we give to it, and about its capacity to help us understand ourselves and our experience of the world we live in. Perhaps also important is learning how it can even give us useful information, allowing us to live more fulfilled lives, individually and collectively. I invite you to hold this same attitude as you review the channeled material that follows. You'll explore channeling's incredible variety next.

CHAPTER 8

Find Your Unique Noetic Signature

My premise is all humans can channel. That everyone can reveal information and energy from beyond time and space. This capacity is something that we are born with.

I am not alone in saying that the capacity for channeling is available to everyone. For instance, take the theories you learned in chapter 5, like the first-sight model and theory. Dr. Currivan (2017) expressed this concept beautifully:

> "By understanding that all that we call reality, not only on the physical plane but also beyond, is consciousness exploring and experiencing itself on myriad levels, the cosmic hologram offers an all-encompassing model of the Cosmos. As the emergence of the cosmic hologram's whole world view expands our perception, it reveals there's essentially nothing that's supernatural or paranormal. Instead, experiences of nonlocal awareness that are capable of transcending space-time, while nonetheless extraordinary, should come to be seen as innate abilities" (197).

Exploring Your Unique Noetic Signature

While we all may have the capacity to channel, that doesn't mean the way we do it is the same. The way you experience channeling is different from the person next to you. Channeling experiences come in all sorts of shapes and sizes. They exist on a spectrum. For example, on one side of the spectrum, there are common, well-studied experiences, like empathy (de Waal and Preston 2017) and intuition (Zander, Ollinger, and Volz 2016). On the other side are perhaps less common experiences, like trance channeling. Most people would say they've experienced a gut hunch or intuition that turned out to be true. Have you?

Multiple studies have looked at the various ways that people experience channeling. For example, the mediums' psychic and mediumistic communication descriptions show that they experience these differently (Beischel, Mosher, and Boccuzzi 2017). The mediums' life histories and expressions of their mediumship can also vary (Beischel, Mosher, and Boccuzzi 2017; Emmons and Emmons 2003). There are many more examples.

The take-home message is that you have a signature for the way you channel that is unique to you. We call this the Noetic Signature. "Noetic" comes from the Greek word *noesis*, which means inner wisdom, direct knowing, intuition, or implicit understanding. What is unique about your Noetic Signature? Rather than comparing ourselves to others, judging who does what better than whom, my invitation is to celebrate the diversity of all of our Noetic Signatures. Through humanity's collective diversity, there is strength. The multidimensional aspects of your Noetic Signature can also be nurtured and strengthened with various techniques.

So, how do you explore the characteristics of your unique Noetic Signature? You can certainly attempt to define it with terms that already exist. Do you experience telepathy, clairvoyance, clairaudience, precognitive dreams, or something else? Likely, you may have experienced more than one type of channeling, and your Noetic Signature is multidimensional. I've seen many people, myself included, struggle with trying to explain how they channel. "Oh, I just know things" could be called claircognizance, which is a category of clairvoyance. But many people wouldn't know what that term means. As you saw in chapter 1, there are many terms and definitions for channeling types. That's not to say that the already-used terms are not useful. They can, however, be limiting and compartmentalizing. Thus, I was inspired to embark on a path to characterize our unique signature in a more encompassing and multidimensional way.

To understand more about the diversity of Noetic Signature, I wanted to start from scratch and not necessarily use the same terms that have been used for a century. I wanted to hear about the lived experiences of many people who channel to see how they directly experience it. We asked over five hundred people to write about how they channel. We explained to the participants what I've been sharing with you in this book: we were interested in ways of knowing beyond our traditional five senses of sight, smell, taste, touch, and hearing. We then looked at all of their answers and came up with common characteristics. This chapter is a summary of what we found. After each section, you'll find some questions that you can answer to assess your own Noetic Signature. Look at each item and record your answers in a journal.

How Do You Engage?

When people described how they channeled, they often began with what they did to get into a channeling space. We call this "ways of engagement." Themes emerged for how people engaged with the process of channeling. The most common ways people engaged in channeling were meditation, intentionally getting into a channeling state, and unintentionally channeling through dreams.

Sometimes I will set a specific intention to channel. Other times information comes to me without me asking for it. This is true for others as well. Channeling can happen on purpose or spontaneously. Most likely, you have also had both intentional and unintentional channeling experiences.

One intentional group of ways people engaged in channeling was internally focused, such as connecting to some force, power, or field greater than themselves. People called this force God, Spirit, Source, Universe, Interconnected Field, Higher Consciousness, Divine, Energy, or other similar terms. Setting an intention to receive information was also very common. You'll learn more about setting intentions in chapters 9 and 10. Related to intention setting was asking or praying to receive information. Other internal processes included meditation, remote viewing, breathwork, astral projection (or purposeful out-of-body experiences), shamanic journeywork, visualization, trance channeling, automatic writing, and lucid dreaming.

Some people used specific external practices, such as being in nature and shamanistic traditions and rituals, including drumming, rattles, music, and dancing. They also used tools such as pendulums, sigils, and so forth, and took substances that induce altered states of consciousness.

Many people also had unintentional, spontaneous channeling experiences. One person shared the following:

I experience a sense of knowing that comes spontaneously and kind of takes me by surprise. There is absolutely no connection to any other thought or information; it doesn't seem logical but always turns out to be

*right. Most of this kind of information is related to people, where I already
have so much information about them in the moment I meet them. It is
like I could see right through them into their soul.*

This is an excellent example of a spontaneous channeling experience.
The person isn't intentionally wanting to know information about the person
they are meeting. It just arrives.

People taking substances to achieve altered states of consciousness also
spontaneously have channeling experiences, even though they did not mean
to. Many unintentional channeling experiences also happen in dreams or
sleep. One person woke from a nightmare in which someone was stealing
their bicycle keys. The next morning, they went outside to find that their
bicycle had actually been stolen! Other people had dreams about major
natural disasters, such as the Japanese tsunami of 2011 or the 6.4 earthquake
in Puerto Rico in 2020. Near-death experiences (NDEs) and OBEs are
another way that people unintentionally have channeling experiences.

How you engage may not necessarily be part of your inherent Noetic Signature. However, learning what motivates you and makes channeling more
accessible to you is vital for nurturing your abilities. I know that meditation,
setting an intention, and being in nature works the best for me. What works
best for you? Here is an assessment to help you explore your own ways of
engagement.

WAYS OF ENGAGEMENT ASSESSMENT

Note in your journal how much you agree or disagree with the following statements, with 0 representing strongly disagree and 100 representing strongly
agree. Average your scores for all the items.

- I have used meditation to access information or energy from
  beyond time and space.

- Being in nature has given me access to noetic information or
  energy.

- I have accessed energy from Earth, spirits, the environment, or
  other forms of nature to receive noetic information.

- I use tools, like pendulums, crystals, or cards, to channel.

- I have used mental imagery to receive information or energy from beyond time and space.

- I have controlled my dreams to gain information or energy from beyond time and space.

- Channeled answers have come to me in my dreams.

- I have woken up from sleep hovering above my body.

- I have had a near-death experience.

- I have had nonphysical beings use my body as a vehicle to communicate verbally.

- My body has been used by nonphysical beings to automatically write or type (automatic writing).

I invite you to notice what makes you more open to channeling experiences in your life. If your experiences are usually spontaneous, see if there are any commonalities to when they happen. If they are intentional, reflect on which methods you find most effective to get you into a channeling state. If your methods are not working as well as you would like, consider experimenting with some of the ways listed above.

Ways of Knowing

Ways of knowing refers to how people can access or reveal information or energy. This was the largest category of responses in our study. Let's review some of the ways people described that they do this. As you read these responses, you may want to keep a journal nearby to write down the ones that resonate with you or that you have experienced. You will also have an opportunity to rate your own channeling experiences at the end of this section.

Intuitive

The most common way of knowing is what many would call intuition. Intuition is the ability to understand something immediately from an instinctive feeling or without the need for conscious reasoning. Here are some of the explanations for this way of knowing: "There is simply a knowing." "I just know it." "It just pops into my head." "It was like the information was just downloaded." "Something that just lights a light bulb of aha." "It is like I just receive these packets of information about a person or situation."

I have heard this idea of "just knowing" from many other sources as well. I experience it too. When you ask someone who "just knows" how they know it, they can't explain it. They just know. The experience is mental. The information just arrives in the mind fully formed, without effort, and often spontaneously.

Embodied

Another prevalent way of knowing is through our bodies. Our bodies are amazingly wonderful and complex. Our bodies are physically sensitive to others' mental intentions (remember the sender-receiver DMILS paradigm I talked about in chapters 4 and 5). Our physiological systems physically change when someone directs their intention toward us. Perhaps our bodies are some kind of psychic antennae.

Similar to how people who know by intuition said, "I just know it," people with embodied aspects of their Noetic Signature said, "I just feel it. I can't say how I feel it. I just do and know it is true." It is not something they know with their mind. It is something they know with their body. They viscerally feel the information.

Many times, the "I just feel it" will appear as a specific sensation in the body. I can't begin to count the number of times I have gotten goosebumps or chills. Not from being cold. For me, goosebumps signal that I am receiving some truth or should continue along the path that was being discussed.

My friend was just sharing with me that they were thinking of moving. They weren't sure where they wanted to move to but had a few places in mind.

I wasn't thinking about channeling for them. I was just being present and actively listening. They mentioned the places they were thinking of. When I heard one of them, my whole body was immediately covered in goosebumps. I interpreted those goosebumps as, "Yes! Explore that city," which is what I shared with my friend. Goosebumps or chills were mentioned by many people in our study.

Others feel cold or hot. Others feel nausea, pain or discomfort, or ill. This is especially true around what they perceive as more negative energy or spirits. Similarly, some people experience dizziness as a sign of channeling. One trance channeler shared that they know their guide wants to connect with them because they feel pressure in their head and slight dizziness.

Some people feel tingles, vibrations, electric, or magnetic type sensations in their bodies. "I know when I have a spirit around me because I get a tingling sensation between my left hip and knee." Others get the typical gut hunch where they physically have a sensation in their stomach. This gut hunch gives them a sign or some information.

Some people describe actually feeling the pain others are experiencing in their own body. Interestingly, when the person realizes that it is not theirs, the pain or discomfort will dissipate. Here are a couple examples:

I was riding in a car with a good friend who had injured her knee in a skiing accident. I knew about the injury, but she didn't go into detail about it. We drove about fifty miles on a scenic drive and then stopped for coffee. I could barely move my right leg, and my right knee hurt like crazy. I asked her if her injured leg was bothering her and which leg it was. She said yes, and it was the right knee. When I realized that it was her physical discomfort I was feeling, the pain and the stiffness in my own leg and knee disappeared.

I am never sick and rarely ever have aches or pains. When I am around others and suddenly have pain, I know it is not mine. I've checked this with people too. I asked one friend, "Steve, do you have a pain behind your left eye, radiating through the temple, and back through under your ear?" He said, "Yes, it's been hurting me all day."

Super Senses

The previous embodied experiences are generalized over your whole body. Other embodied channeling is perceived to be related to our senses. Just as you have your five traditional senses, some people experience "super" versions of their five senses.

SEEING

Many people "see" inner visions or images in their minds when they channel, like in this example:

Sometimes the information is a flash of visual awareness, sometimes instantaneously, almost before the question is formed. One time my husband misplaced his keys. He was looking all over for them. All of a sudden, I "saw" them hidden under some papers in the bottom drawer of his office desk. When I gave him this information, he returned to work and went exactly to the spot I had described. Sure enough, he found the keys hidden from view under a bunch of papers in his desk drawer.

The information shows up as a picture in their mind's eye. Remote viewing, which we've talked about previously, is another example of inner seeing.

Outer seeing is a less common experience. This refers to you seeing things in your surroundings that are not ordinarily visible with your physical eyes. You might see lights and colors around others, your recently passed loved ones in after-death communications, or other nonphysical beings, like guides and angels. Angel or other-worldly visitations are present throughout human history in many world religions. For example, Joseph Smith, the founder of the Latter-Day Saints, apparently saw beings who directed his founding of the church.

HEARING

People hearing an inner voice has been discussed throughout recorded history. Apparently, Socrates had an inner voice that often gave him warning messages to protect him. One time it told him not to walk down a particular street in Athens. He heeded the message and went a different way. His friends did not follow him and were knocked down by a heard of pigs (Hastings 1991, 119). Researcher Alfred Alschuler, inspired by hearing his own inner voices, reviewed historical figures who heard inner voices. He found 150 individuals who heard inner voices, such as Martin Luther and Saint Teresa (Hastings 1991, 121).

Hearing an inner voice was commonly reported in our study. Many of these messages happened spontaneously to protect from danger like Socrates's warning.

> I have had experiences of hearing a voice warning me not to go to a certain address in my working service. As I was traveling to patients' homes, I would occasionally "hear" a voice that was not my own give me a short important message to follow, like "Don't go there now." I followed that message. When I went there later, the police were there and had arrested someone for robbing people in the lobby of that building.

Not all messages are related to danger or decisions that need to be made. Other participants expressed receiving insight, creative ideas, and additional useful information through their inner voice. Of course, professional psychics and mediums can have extended conversations with their inner voice. One study of people who identified themselves as psychic practitioners found that 91 percent of them had an inner voice. They also found the messages from this voice positive and helpful (Hastings 1991, 121).

TOUCH

People described two ways that touch shows up in their Noetic Signature. One is through touching objects. Some people can touch an item and gain information about its owner or other information that one would not usually know.

> I can pick up information by touch alone, and this has taken me back in time through the life events experienced by that object to its creation. For example, I can trace the life of a carved crystal right back to its formation in the earth and receive images of all the places, people, and situations that crystal has been through, including the vibration of carving.

This was also common in people working in healing therapies where touch is involved. A massage therapist may touch a person and get information about a person's emotions, life situation, and past traumas.

Another aspect of touch is feeling nonphysical beings. Some people seem to be more sensitive to feeling nonphysical beings. They may not see or hear them but can feel the nonphysical beings touching them.

SMELLING AND TASTING

Super smell and taste senses are not as common but do happen. For example, a person might suddenly smell roses in a closed room in their home where they could not possibly be smelling roses. This smell then brings to mind a deceased family member who loved roses. When they sense the roses, they feel that their deceased loved one must be nearby. Here is a fascinating example:

> One time, I suddenly smelled my niece's vomit—very intense and disgusting. I then searched my home for signs that someone was sick only to find that no one was. At the same time, I received a knowing that this smell was connected to my sister who lives a great distance away, across many states. Sure enough, about twenty minutes later, I received a phone call from my sister explaining that she'd been at the movies when her daughter got sick and she was in the restroom holding back her hair while she vomited into the toilet.

Experiences of taste not related to the physical are even more unusual but also happen. In one example, someone described how they have a way of "tasting" energy. When they contemplate future ideas, they get a taste in the back of their throat that gives them information about their decision.

Emotions

Another way people know things is through emotions. Empathy is a standard human capacity. Understanding or feeling what another person is going through from their perspective is part of being a loving, caring human. However, many people experience empathy on a different level beyond this ordinary capacity. They can actually feel other people's emotions directly.

Star Trek: The Next Generation was one of my favorite shows in the '90s. Deanna is the starship's counselor and an empath. She can sense other people's emotions. In many episodes, the starship's captain will ask for her insight into the feelings and intent of the many unique characters they meet from around the galaxy. Deanna is also negatively affected when she is around people who are suffering or when disasters strike and many people are traumatically killed. I believe Deanna's character has normalized empathic abilities. In the last couple of decades, since the show aired, the concept that people are sensitive to emotions has become commonplace.

Here are some more examples from the "real" world:

I am an empath. I feel energy viscerally in my body. For example, when others feel strong emotions, particularly grief, I feel the same emotions within myself. I can feel in my body before someone will cry.

I don't like being in large crowds as I am so aware of everyone else's feelings. Sometimes I will draw from the collective energies in the crowd to give me the strength to just be there and sustain the bombardment of the emotions.

If channeled emotions are a prominent part of your Noetic Signature, learning to distinguish between your feelings and any channeled emotions is essential. It can support you in being more emotionally balanced. Many people realize that the feelings they are experiencing are not even theirs! Once they learn tools to clear these emotions, they are more emotionally resilient. You will learn about clearing techniques to help you clear feelings that are not yours from your system in chapter 10.

Direct

Another way of knowing is direct. In direct ways of knowing, the information comes from something, someone, or somewhere else. For example, information can be directly received from animals, the environment, deceased people, and other nonphysical beings, like spirits, guides, and other entities. Getting information directly from other beings, spirits, or entities was one of the most common ways of knowing in general and the most common direct way of knowing.

Often the messages from the deceased happen in dreams. The loved one will give a message that is specific to the dreaming person or a message to pass on to another person. I find the most exciting messages are the ones where the deceased person tells the loved one about a missing or lost item. The loved one can then find that object. Pictures falling down, radios turning on, objects being displaced, and other physical manifestations are credited to deceased loved ones too. Spiritual guides, angels, spirits, and other entities are also reported to give direct information that a person needs.

Numerous people expressed being able to directly get information from others' thoughts or intentions and even animals' minds. People also said they got information directly from living people. For example, one participant had to make a decision. They internally asked the Universe what they should do. Within ten minutes, someone came up to them and said something that was totally relevant to the choice they needed to make.

People feel they know things through symbols that appear to them. The repetition of a particular or unusual symbol may keep appearing that has meaning to the person.

Another way I appear to receive information is via things that happen in my external world, such as the same symbol being shown to me over and over. Last year when my mother was in the hospital, the number nineteen kept presenting itself repeatedly. My mother even noticed the strangeness associated with all the coincidences surrounding this number. It was as if someone was trying to tell me something.

People directly knew energy and information as it moved through their body too. Sometimes they received direct information from the energy and information. Other times, they would need to interpret what the energy or information meant. For example, imagine walking into a room and reading the "energy" and knowing what happened there before you arrived. Another example is feeling an energy surge through your body that invigorated and recharged you. You felt changed by the experience but didn't necessarily receive any specific information about what happened.

There is no one right way of knowing. In fact, most people experience many different types of channeled knowing. Intuitive, embodied, "super" senses, emotions, and direct are the various significant themes that arose for people in our Noetic Signature survey. Looking at the multiple ways of knowing themes, inner visions, "just knowing," inner voices, and "just feel it" were the top ways people talked about. What about you? What are your main ways of knowing? You can use the assessment below to explore your Noetic Signature.

WAYS OF KNOWING ASSESSMENT

Note in your journal how much you agree or disagree with the following statements, with 0 representing strongly disagree and 100 representing strongly agree. Average your scores for each subcategory.

Intuitive

- I have "just known" possible truths about people or situations.
- I have known things about myself, others, or places that come true in the future.
- I have had channeled information just "pop into my head."

Embodied

- I have just felt in my body when something is true or not.
- I have known I was getting channeled information or energy when I suddenly felt cold for no reason.
- Goosebumps have been a sign that I'm receiving channeled information that I should listen to.
- Feeling heat in my body has been a sign that I'm getting channeled information.
- I have found that physical pain or discomfort in my body relates to channeled energy or information.
- I have known information about people, places, and situations through a physical "gut feeling."

- Channeled information has come to me through tingles, vibrations, electric energy, or magnetic energy in my body.
- I have tuned in to my body's physical sensations to receive guidance or information about my life decisions.

Super senses

- I've seen things in my environment like spirits or lights around people.
- I have heard the sounds or voices of spirits or other nonphysical beings around me.
- I have seen things in my mind's eye that provide me with information or energy from beyond time and space.
- I have heard noetic information internally like an "inner voice."
- I have smelled spirits or other nonphysical beings.
- Channeled information has come to me in the form of unusual tastes in my mouth that are unrelated to food or drink.
- I have felt someone or something that was not physically present "touch" me.
- I have gained information I wouldn't usually know through touching objects.

Emotions

- I have felt emotions that aren't about me but tell me things about other people, places, or times.
- I have experienced noetic information or energy through my emotions.

Direct

- Connecting with animals is one way I have received noetic information.

- I have received guidance from entities that are not of this world.

- I have communicated with or channeled information from deceased people.

- Tuning in to my environment has been a source of noetic energy or information for me.

- I have communicated with nonhuman beings, such as spirits, entities, or spirit guides.

- I have just known things about people upon meeting them, without even talking to them.

- I have received information directly from the energy of the Universe.

- I have experienced a palpable nonphysical energy moving through my body.

- Noetic information has appeared to me in symbols (shapes, designs, or images that signify some meaning).

What did you notice about your Noetic Signature? How you experience your ways of knowing is unique to you. There is no right or wrong way to do it. There is also no better or worse way to do it. Your way of knowing is just that: your way of knowing. Your way of knowing is precisely as it needs to be right now.

You'll continue to explore how to nurture your Noetic Signature in chapter 10. Next, you'll learn about another channeling theme we found in our survey related to channeling experiences.

Ways of Affecting

You can understand ways of knowing as a receptive activity. Many of the experiences you've just learned about are called "receptive psi." Channeling experiences in which people influence their world, such as psychokinesis (or mind over matter), are called "expressive psi." This influence, or "ways of affecting," was another central theme that we analyzed in people's responses about channeling. These experiences have to do with affecting the world around us, such as through healing, decision making, influencing others, and influencing the environment with our mind or intentions.

Healing

Healing the self and others was commonly expressed. Using our intention, energy, thoughts, and manifestation, whatever you want to call it, to heal. You can think of this as a form of mind over matter. Some of these examples are quite remarkable and unexplainable by normal means.

> I healed my stage IV cancer by bringing healing light/energy into me (from the Creator) and visualizing it healing my tumor, by aligning my EM [electromagnetic] energy with the planet, and by creating a state of grateful energy.

> I was near someone who had a bruise or illness and described it. I have watched as their bruise or illness dissipates, and I suddenly have the bruise in the same spot, or illness. (I avoid sick people.)

Decision Making

Another very common comment—in fact, one of the top ten most common comments—was that the information supported them in making decisions in their lives. For example, people remarked that they could receive information about upcoming events in their lives and then change their behavior based on the information they received.

> I often will ask my "beings" for guidance—it may be a yes-no to something such as, Is it good to visit today? I generally will often get a very clear yes or no to things, and I have found that if I follow this, things go well, but if I go against this, which I very rarely do now (it's usually just that I forgot to ask and check in), that things do not go well. I use this for guidance around many things: planning work things, food, what is good for me at times, social things, and so forth.

Many people described how powerful their channeling experiences were for their own self-growth. The information or energy they received supported a deeper self-awareness, introspection, or reflection for the respondents.

Influencing Others

Some people also experience their thoughts affecting someone else or influencing others somehow, like being in the same dream with another person, influencing someone within a dream, and synchronistic connections across time and space.

In 1986, I was stuck in a job that I didn't like as a bookkeeper. What I really wanted was to work as a bookkeeper with an accountant whom I'd worked with a couple of years previously. I did not contact her directly. Instead, I placed a thought "out there" (wherever "there" is) that she should contact me. Four days later, she called and offered me a job.

The above experience is a similar concept of visualization or manifestation that was frequently mentioned. This also aligns with the idea of goal-directed results you saw in many laboratory studies. Many people talked about visualizing something they wanted to have happen and then observing it manifest at some point in the immediate future.

One important thing to note is that others' influence can be used with ill will or harmful intent. A few people said they used their intention to harm others. Some spiritual traditions discourage aspirants from exploring channeling "superpowers" for this very reason. A spiritually immature person may become distracted by the abilities or use them to harm.

In fact, some channeled material says that channeling abilities are being blocked in some way because humanity can't handle them yet. Humanity is apparently not spiritually mature enough to handle the responsibility required to channel. Imagine the destruction and havoc that could be caused by people using telepathic powers for ill will. You see these fears depicted in many of our superhero movies. These "powers" are not good or bad in and of themselves. You get to choose how you want to use them.

Influencing Systems, Objects, and the Environment

Extensive research shows that our intention can influence physical objects. In chapters 4 and 5, we reviewed the numerous random number generator laboratory studies showing this. Our intention affects physical objects outside the lab also. Here's a great example:

> As an experiment, I wanted free electricity. I went to sleep with the intention to stop the meter from turning. In a dream that night, I was able to put my mind inside the meter. When I awoke, I remembered the dream instantly and was very excited. I got dressed barely containing my excitement, ran outside, and saw that the meter was stopped. I asked my kids to turn the central air [conditioning] on and then off again, [to see if the electric meter would move] and there was no movement on the meter. I had free electricity for two months except for a base-charge minimum. I got worried that the electric company would come out and change the meter, so I went outside and put my hand on it. I asked my son to turn the central air off and on again. I removed my hand, and the meter was turning again.

Healing yourself or others, affecting others, and influencing systems, objects, or your environment are examples of how people experience their intentions affecting the physical world in an expressive way. You can look at the items below to see how prominent ways of affecting are in your Noetic Signature.

WAYS OF AFFECTING ASSESSMENT

Note in your journal how much you agree or disagree with the following statements, with 0 representing strongly disagree and 100 representing strongly agree. Average your scores for all the items. See how they compare to the Ways of Knowing section.

- I have shared with others the noetic messages I have received about them.

- I have impacted other people by focusing my energy or thoughts on them.

- My intentions have impacted my surrounding environment.

- Others have reported feeling healed after I have done energy work with them.

- I have used energy or information from beyond space and time to heal myself.

- I have used information from beyond space and time to make decisions in my life.

- I have used my intention to affect objects in the physical world.

- I have sent information to other people with my mind.

- The noetic information or energy I have received affects how I view myself.

You have likely experienced a least one of these ways of knowing and ways of affecting channeling experiences at some point in your life. Perhaps you have experienced more than one. Some may have resonated with you, and others may have seemed like science fiction.

We are wonderfully diverse. Your channeling experiences are unique to you. Your ability for some types may be greater than for others. That does not mean that someone who can use their mind to affect physical objects is better than someone who is intuitive and gets gut hunches occasionally. They are just different. Your Noetic Signature is distinctive, unique, and special. Your Noetic Signature brings its specific "frequency" to the magnificent whole. I invite you to be open and curious about your Noetic Signature and its current characteristics. These may change over time. In chapter 10, you will explore how to nurture your Noetic Signature if you choose.

CHAPTER 9

Use Your Intention to Direct the Content

Setting intentions is a powerful way to direct your channeling experience and discover the relevance and meaning of channeled material for you. Intention setting is the process of focusing your undivided attention and your will toward a particular objective, aim, or plan. Intention setting is like telling the Universe what you would like your life to align with and letting the Universe figure out exactly how and when that will happen. One example of intention is, "My intention is to clear any obstacles blocking me from channeling."

An intention is different from a goal. A goal could be, "I will do my channeling practice every day for five minutes." It is specific and measurable. You often have direct control over making it happen. Intentions, on the other hand, don't have expectations or evaluations attached to them. You are just declaring the outcome that you envision. You aren't defining exactly how your outcome will happen. Another example of intention is, "My intention is to feel more joy in my workday." You can use intentions for any aspect of your life. They are essential for learning and developing your channeling abilities.

One way you can use intention is to decide whether the information you receive from channeling is relevant for you. This is important because not all channeled material may be useful to you. I and others have found that some channeled material is nonsensical, redundant, or irrelevant. Some communicators can seem to have their own agendas and desires not related to the channeler or audience. Some even appear to be deceptive. Some provide unreliable information and do not take responsibility for the implications of the material (Hastings 1991, 169).

Some people believe that any channeled material is true and relevant to them just because it is channeled. This is not true. I am not sharing this to scare you. However, it is essential to use your judgment and intuition to decide if the material is right for you. In essence, you can't take channeled material at its face value. You must choose when and how to use channeled material in your life. This is true regardless of what you think the source is, the type of information that comes through, or how it arrives. Discernment is key. Intention setting can help you decide what material is relevant and meaningful for your life.

Practicing Discernment

There is no one right way to discern the relevance of channeled material for you. I invite you to explore what path is right for you. Here is one practice to start with that can help you develop your own discernment method.

DISCERNMENT EXERCISE

Find a place to sit where you are comfortable and relaxed. Take some deep breaths. Wiggle your toes and feel your feet on the floor. Feel your body resting against whatever you are sitting on. Quiet your mind as best you can, perhaps imagining a clear blue sky. Set the intention for your highest and best self to be revealed. Set the intention that you will receive clear answers and guidance to your questions.

Then, bring to mind the channeled information you want to assess. Ask yourself the following questions, as they are relevant to you and your situation. Use yes-no answers to start. If other items come to you, ask them as well.

Feel into your body after you ask each question. Do you feel contracted or expanded? Do you receive an internal auditory yes or no? Do you receive an image or a symbol that represents yes or no to you?

Trust your intuition. If you feel contracted for most of the answers, then perhaps the message is not for you. If you feel an expansion or received other signs of a yes, then explore the relevance of the information for your life. Don't get caught up in whether the situation or person giving the information is not real or fake or a fraud. Just focus on its relevance to you and your process.

- Is the source of this information important for me to know?

- If yes, what is the source of this information?

- Is this information relevant to my life?

- Is this information something that I should implement or integrate into my life?

- Will this information support me on my path in some way?

- Is there anything else I need to know about this information?

- If yes, what is it?

When you feel like the process is done, end your session with an offer of gratitude—to yourself, to the process, to whatever inspires you.

There is no right or wrong way to practice discernment. Just setting the intention for discernment will often clarify whether the information is useful for you or not. You can repeat this process as many times as you want and for any channeling experience. This process can also happen very quickly. Once you get used to a discernment method that works for you, you can do it in a few minutes or even a few seconds for more straightforward cases. We all have the capacity to tune in to our intuition in this way.

Here is a typical example of a channeling that was meaningful for the channeler in making a decision:

Lisa was deciding whether she should start a sewing home business. She was agonizing over her decision. She reviewed the marketing and advertising she'd need to do, the finances, including how much she'd have to generate to survive, and the types of sewing services she could provide. She even reached out to friends and professionals about whether it was the right decision or not. Even after going over all this information, she was incredibly stressed about her decision. She was not sleeping well, and the stress of the decision was negatively affecting her health. One night in desperation, she asked for guidance from her deceased father. She mentally reached out to him, asking whether it was the right decision for her to open her business or not. She asked him to give her a clear sign. That night, she had a dream. She saw her father standing in their favorite park. He looked toward her, gave her a big smile, nodded his head, and gave her two thumbs-up. When Lisa awoke in the morning, she was ecstatic to have received a message from her father. She felt a great sense of calm, peace, and knowingness that she should move forward with her home business.

Did Lisa's message really come from her deceased father? Or was it her higher self? Or maybe it was her unconscious mind that integrated all the information she had researched into a symbol that she would see as a green light to move forward. We don't know the source of this channeled message. It could have been Lisa's deceased father, her higher self, and her unconscious mind that integrated all her researched information into a dream symbol, or it could have been something else entirely. Regardless, Lisa felt clear about the meaning of the message. She felt expanded and had the clarity she hadn't felt before. Lisa's channeled message was meaningful to her, and it helped her move forward in her life.

Many people benefit from channeled information. Of course, our major world religions have channeled messages at their core. Participation in religion and spirituality supports longer life and reduced rates of heart, digestive, and lung disease; dementia; cancer; inflammation; and high cholesterol. People participating in religious and spiritual practices also rate their health and well-being higher than those who don't (Oman 2018).

Beyond the impact of religion and spirituality, channeling can improve physical, emotional, and spiritual health. Here are just a couple examples. There are many more. The channeled curriculum *A Course in Miracles* is a complete, self-study, universal, spiritual thought system that has supported numerous people on their personal growth path. Mediumship has also helped people in their grief process. People who had a mediumship session received a sign, message, or other contact with their deceased loved one. These sessions buoyed them emotionally and had a positive impact on their grieving process. It even positively affected the resolution of their grief (Beischel, Mosher, and Boccuzzi 2015; Beischel 2019). Eighty-three participants in one study were asked to rate their grief before and after a mediumship session. On average, their grief levels were reduced (Beischel 2014; Beischel, Mosher, and Boccuzzi 2015). Dr. Julie Beischel and Mark Boccuzzi continue this critical work in their bereavement and mediumship (BAM) research at the Windbridge Institute.

Messages about what to do in our lives, like Lisa's, are pervasive. This is just one of many types of information that come through channeling. If you can think of a topic, material has been channeled about it. While the quality varies widely, I would challenge you to find a topic that does not have channeled material on it. Volumes and volumes of channeled material exist around the world. Let's review some of the most common topics that are seen repeatedly and see how they could be relevant for you: guidance and personal messages, ageless wisdom, descriptions of life in nonphysical realms, the past or the future, artistic and creative expression, scientific or technological material, health, healing, and information from or about deceased humans (Klimo 1998, 176–191). As you read through the summaries, ask yourself if these types of messages resonate with you.

Guidance and Personal Messages

What should I do about my job? What should I do about my son's behavior? Where should we move to? These are the types of questions that get answered in this content category. The answers can show up in many ways, like suddenly "just knowing" the answer, getting goosebumps when thinking about a way to act, getting a download of information, or getting information from dreams. Professional channelers are often asked for guidance and personal messages. Information in this category can help you decide or shift your emotions, thoughts, or behavior somehow.

If you receive this type of information from channeling, you are not alone. Guidance and personal messages are the most common material people say they receive whether they are trance channelers or scientists or engineers. Sometimes the information is precise to the person, but other times it can be general.

You are more than your physical body. This is a common general theme that people receive, especially through mediums and trance channelers. For example, Dr. Hunter interviewed many trance channelers and physical mediums at the Bristol Spirit Lodge in Bristol, UK. He collated the content and found a similar theme: "the idea that consciousness can survive the death of the physical body, that personhood is partible, that the body is permeable, that reality is nonphysical, and that the consciousness is a fundamental property of the universe" (Hunter 2014, 113–114).

Understanding your true nature then helps you "wake up." Your waking up then helps humanity awaken. The messages are abundant. All you need to do is type in "channeled message" and "awaken humanity" to see the many listings of this same "personal" message.

With many channeling experiences, directly experiencing a phenomenon goes much further for understanding it than learning about it. Interestingly, communicators from our studies said that you should use direct experience as "proof" to understand the "we are all one" message. If you have a direct experience of oneness, then you do not necessarily need "proof."

Awakening humanity one person at a time seems like a tall order. Balancing your masculine and feminine aspects is one specific guidance for how to do this. First, you acknowledge that you have both a feminine and masculine aspect, regardless of your gender or gender identity.

> *We are all both. You just wear different outfits. Until you as individuals have the balance within you to love and honor and cherish each part of you, you will not reach the love and peace that humanity needs to achieve.*

Then, you can do a practice to balance your masculine and feminine energies. I experienced this reconciliation process for myself before hearing that message. It was an incredible process that left me in a state of profound peace and bliss. You can explore balancing your masculine and feminine aspects if it is right for you with this channeled practice.

Practice knowing yourself through meditation if you wish. Sit quietly and ask for the masculine and feminine parts of you to come forth. They will come forth. Let them introduce themselves to you. Become familiar with the male part of you and the female part of you. Make peace with both parts because through time with your own experience, one is stronger than the other, or the human part of you fears one or the other. Practice becoming aware of those parts. And if you bring those parts forth, let them talk to each other while you observe. Journal about your experience with this exercise.

The synthesis of different parts of us is not a new concept. Robert Assagioli created a process to integrate various aspects of ourselves, called psychosynthesis.[38] This work aims to integrate the different aspects of ourselves into a purposeful personality, connect to our higher self, and realize the spiritual self, moving from self-identity to a transpersonal understanding of oneself (Hastings 1991, 89).

Because this is the most common channeled content category, you will likely receive specific or general guidance and personal messages for living your life through your own channeling or from others. Awakening humanity, our true nature not being limited by our physical bodies, and balancing our masculine and feminine aspects are just a few topics in this channeled content category.

Ageless Wisdom

Channeled transcripts are full of content on ageless wisdom present at the core of many of our world religions. Ageless wisdom—concepts like "We are all one," the existence of multidimensional beings and realms, universal interconnectedness, and the power of your thoughts—is the second most common content category for trance channelers, and the third most common for general channelers.

Concepts like "We are all one" and "Everything is an aspect of this larger all that is" embody the "perennial philosophy," a term coined in the sixteenth century. The perennial philosophy proposes that there are core truths to all experiences of spirituality, mysticism, philosophies, and religions of the world and across the age, even though they appear different on the surface (Randrup 2003; Ferrer 2000; Celenza 2017). Teachers for millennia have been giving messages of love, peace, harmony, forgiveness, and reciprocity.

> *All of creation is oneness. There is no separation. We all are you. And you are all us.*

Judith Skutch commented that "the same perennial philosophy or ancient wisdom [is] expressed through different voices" (Klimo 1998, 175). Judith's insight that there was a similar message coming through multiple voices aligns with my experience. In our Mount Shasta focus groups, a communicator was asked why multiple channelers worldwide were channeling the same being, such as Jesus or Archangel Michael. The response was that the same message is distributed in as many ways as possible to make sure the message is received. Apparently, the channeler, message, listener, and communicator all have "frequencies" that combine uniquely. Someone listening to channeler A with the same message may not really hear the message in the same way they would if they heard it from channeler B. This explains why you might hear the same messages over and over again in different ways.

People also experience this oneness directly through channeling. Here is an example from our noetic signature study:

> *Everything I access feels intelligent and conscious, and I have been told by "spirit" numerous times that everything is consciousness and love.*

One other ageless wisdom message you may have heard is that Earth and humanity are part of an interconnected Universe, that our planet is not isolated but part of a larger whole, and more importantly, that what happens on our planet affects the rest of our Universe. Apparently, humanity's thoughts are experienced beyond Earth.

> *This entire Universe is related to this planet and everything. Yes, and that means every thought you think, every word you say, and every action you take can be felt through the entire Universe and multiverse, and humans will awaken more and more to this fact and to its implications of interconnectedness.*

This quote means that your thoughts influence not only those around you but the entire Universe. The idea that your thoughts affect the Universe is overwhelming. The implications are that your thoughts have consequences. Imagine what your world would be like if others could quickly know what you were thinking! Or if your thoughts were immediately manifested tangibly. Science fiction stories abound with this idea. "I can fly," says the main character, and suddenly the person is flying through the air. You likely don't see this in your life today in such a tangible and immediate way.

We do see it in other, less direct ways. You saw the Global Consciousness Project results and numerous random number generator projects showing you that thoughts do, in fact, affect the physical world. This idea is also mirrored in many spiritual traditions.

You could easily get overwhelmed by this idea or feel powerless by it. You are not alone. Now that you are aware of your thoughts' power, you can take action if you choose to. Meditation and mindfulness programs teach and train people to become aware of their thoughts. One such program is Mindfulness-Based Stress Reduction by Jon Kabat-Zinn. In the course, you learn that your thoughts are just mental events moving through your mind. You understand that you are not your thoughts. You learn how to observe your thoughts without getting caught up in them. Most meditation training includes some practice for strengthening your awareness of your thoughts.

Descriptions of Life in Other Physical and Nonphysical Realms

There are nonphysical multidimensional beings and realms that you can't usually see, which make up another common content category. You have likely heard of these in our oldest recorded histories and myths about our ancestors, angels, teachers, or nature spirits. The Western materialistic paradigm dismisses these beings as myths or from our imaginations. Despite this dismissal, channeled content matches many ancient stories of visitations, guidance, and other connections with multidimensional nonphysical beings throughout time. This category was the third most common with trance channelers in our surveys and almost last with general channelers. I think this is so because, as we saw in chapter 7, a common supposed source of trance channeling is multidimensional beings. You would imagine they have something to say about their worlds.

Our Mount Shasta focus group with trance channelers supposedly had communicators hailing from other parts of the galaxy, such as the Pleiades, Sirius, Arcturus, and Orion. The communicators discussed how they communicate, their physical form, galactic distance and time travel, and other galactic civilizations' role in the creation and evolution of humanity.

Some of these communicators described what their worlds were like: "Our world feels like love, celebration, upliftment, and the constant eagerness to learn and teach." They described their "body" as similar to a star, like a vibration with balanced masculine and feminine aspects. They said they communicate with each other telepathically but not with words. They use packets of information or "blocks of thought."

In the future, humans will apparently be able to see these nonphysical beings with our physical eyes. When we asked communicators when this would happen, they said:

When the love vibration is high enough, because they only can appear in a vibration of love and joy and no other vibration, they will begin to appear gradually to individuals. The first step was the starships, the physical starships that we can see. That was a very big step for more and more to see...the ones who have reached the highest levels of love and joy will be capable to see them in the physical.

Interestingly, other mediumistic communications and near-death experience reports give similar descriptions of life in nonphysical realms. Near-death experiences have common aspects, like a guiding light, a tunnel, meeting someone the person knowns or other loving nonphysical beings, and life reviews (Kean 2018; van Lommel et al. 2001; Alexander 2012; Fontana 2009).

You may find some of this material fantastical. Or perhaps you have had a direct experience of nonphysical beings and this material resonates with you. I find the material useful because it expands my mind to think that we are not alone in the Universe. I always found it unbelievable that Earth was the only habitable planet. At this point, it seems that only time will tell whether these other physical and nonphysical worlds are fully revealed in our lifetime. In the meantime, you can use your discernment practice to decide how relevant the information is to you in your daily life.

The Past and the Future

Fascinating information has been channeled about the past and the future. In our surveys, this topic was the second most common in general channelers and the fourth most common in trance channelers. In our Noetic Signature survey, knowing information about the future was the second most common channeling experience.

Ancient civilizations, like Atlantis and Lemuria, have been spoken about by numerous channelers but have yet to be verified. Other channeled information about the past has been verified, including archaeological sites' locations using remote viewing (Schwartz 2005).

Channeled prophecy of what our future might hold has also been reported through recorded history. From 1978 to 1996, Schwartz asked over four thousand people worldwide and in various professions the same questions about the year 2050. By overwhelming consensus, the vision of our future world is very different from the world today. Apparently, there will be no overpopulation, a new form of decentralized energy, no chronic illness or money, and the

United States will not exist as it presently does. Interestingly, the participants shared many things that can actually be verified already: the disappearance of the Soviet Union, no nuclear war, the rise of climate change, the flooding of coastal cities, massive migrations, the decline of carbon energy transportation, business meetings with people geographically separated that are carried out through a form of video conferencing, the collapse of antibiotic medicine, and the rise of superbugs. They also saw a series of epidemics, the first being a blood disease that crossed over from primates to humans in Africa that would spread worldwide, killing millions (Schwartz 2017). Perhaps COVID-19 is the second. Schwartz is working on a similar project, asking people about their remote viewings about the year 2060.

These examples reflect the distant past and future. Many channeling experiences provide information about the imminent future. Here is a dramatic example:

I was sitting at a stoplight with a large truck stopped next to me in the left turn lane. It was completely blocking my view to the left. It was winter, the windows were closed, and the heat was on, masking outside noise. The light turned green, and I sat there for a couple of seconds (and usually I am quick off the mark!) because I knew for sure that a huge truck would come barreling through the intersection from the left at high speed. That is exactly what happened. If I had followed my normal course of action, I would have almost certainly been killed.

I can't imagine what it would have been like to be this person. How many times have you been saved from some dangerous situation by heeding your intuition, whether consciously or unconsciously? In this case, it was evident to the person what was happening. This might be happening without you even knowing. Here's another example:

I've also had a few precognitive events, where I unexpectedly got a quick vision or knowingness (almost like a snapshot) of something that was going to happen. One afternoon when I was about thirteen years old, I was home alone and got flashes of something really bad happening to my parents. I was sure they were going to die. These flashes of knowingness came at the same time that they were in a serious car accident. They survived but were both injured and hospitalized for a period of time.

This is another dramatic example. But these are not isolated examples; there were so many stories like this from our five hundred respondents. The number of warning messages were incredible. Perhaps channeling can give you a glimpse of a probable reality, allowing you to maybe shift your behavior to encourage or prevent it. The notion of a guardian angel whispering or sometimes yelling in our ear to protect us comes to mind. Spiritualist traditions believe that we have a spirit guide or other nonphysical beings who watch over, protect, and help us in our life. These examples certainly support this idea.

You can receive channeled information about the past, immediate future, or distant future. Perhaps the most relevant messages are ones that warn you about some imminent danger. Strengthening your discernment and channeling abilities will help you notice these messages more clearly and respond to them appropriately.

Health and Healing

Health and healing were the fourth most common content category in our general channelers and fifth in the trance channelers. It is also a common concern for people reaching out to mediums, psychics, and channelers. You may have reached out to someone about this yourself. Stories of miraculous healings stir wonder in all of us. Numerous accounts of health and healing have crossed my path. Here is a remarkable one of many stories:

> I was part of a healing circle at church. A toddler had an inoperable brain tumor. The whole church connected by touching and focusing on healing the innocent child. I saw the energy, like a golden web, lines extending from one person to another to another, then flowing into the child. Two weeks later, his doctors were extremely confused…there was no tumor, no cancer, just a healthy child.

Amazingly, stories like these are not unusual. The Institute of Noetic Sciences published an extensive bibliography cataloging spontaneous remission cases like this reported in the medical literature (Wahbeh 2020; O'Regan and Hirshberg 1993). Many of these could be attributed to some channeling phenomenon. The bibliography contains more than thirty-five hundred references from more than eight hundred journals in twenty different languages. These do not even include cases like the above that are not written up in a medical journal. IONS Fellow Dr. Joshua Weiss and team are currently updating the bibliography with spontaneous remission cases from 1993 to the present.

These are just a few examples of seemingly miraculous healing, where our intention or mind influenced matter. Obviously, this is an area of channeling experience that could dramatically benefit you. You can use your channeling to choose things in your daily life that support your health. Health and healing is one area where there are clear, practical applications for you. You can use your channeling to find out the best foods for you to eat, the best exercise for your body, or what is causing you to not sleep so well. You could also experience energy medicine modalities, such as Reiki or Therapeutic Touch, that have growing evidence for their benefit, which I categorize as a form of channeling. More and more research and attention are being directed toward energy medicine and its potential.

Information From or About Deceased Humans

This is probably the most well-known channeled information type. It wasn't the most common noted for our trance or general channelers, but it is undoubtedly the most publicized. Numerous research studies have explored the work of mediums who claim they access information or directly channel deceased humans. Psychic services, many of which are people seeking to speak with deceased loved ones, are estimated to earn about $2 billion in annual sales in the United States (IBISWorld 2019). But communications during a session aren't the only ones you can have.

An after-death communication, or ADC, is when a person is directly and spontaneously contacted by someone who has died (Guggenheim and Guggenheim 2012). ADCs can take many forms. For example, you can feel a "presence" or see the person with your physical eyes. Many times you might see a person who has just died without knowing that they passed yet. Sometimes these experiences can be upsetting for people, especially if they happen spontaneously and are unexpected. For the most part, people who have ADCs are glad that they happened and gain some positive meaning from them.

Whether through mediumship, trance channeling, or ADCs, people say that what they receive is from or about people who have died. As you saw in previous chapters, the belief in life after death and contact with the dead is widespread worldwide. If this has happened to you, you are definitely not alone.

Art and Science

Artistic and creative expression and scientific discoveries were less commonly noted as content categories in our surveys. That being said, there is no end to the artistic and creative expressions that people have said were channeled somehow. You could say that the creative process itself is an intuitive, channeled experience. You saw the incredible examples of channeled artistic material like José Andrade's landscapes, still lifes, and portraits; Luiz Antônio Gasparetto's paintings; Rosemary Brown's piano compositions; and Pearl Curran's literary excellence. Many who create have shared with me and others that they didn't know where their work came from. They get some insight and inspiration and start working at a feverish pitch until they've completed their work of art. William Blake, visionary, artist, and poet, commented that his literary works would arrive fully formed (Blake 1803).

Similarly, many scientific breakthroughs have been attributed to channeling (Schwartz 1995). Friedrich Kekulé was a German chemist who was struggling with the structure of benzene, a six-carbon organic compound. He had a daydream of an ouroboros, which is a snake grabbing its own tail. This symbol inspired his thinking about benzene, from which he discovered its cyclical structure (Benfey 1958). Srinivasa Ramanujan was a brilliant mathematician who believed some of his concepts were channeled by Indian deities. Nikola Tesla was walking in a park when he suddenly had a vision that led to the invention of the electric motor (Rakovic 2010).

Most of us also know the story of how Isaac Newton discovered the idea of gravity. He was sitting in his garden in meditation. He saw an apple fall off of a tree. From that, he came to the idea of a universal force of gravity (McKie and De Beer, 1951). Other scientists have commented that their remarkable ideas do not originate with them—that they receive them from something outside of themselves. Thomas Edison said, "People say I have created things.

I have never created anything. I get impressions from the Universe at large and work them out, but I am only a plate on a record or a receiving apparatus—what you will. Thoughts are really impressions that we get from outside" (Dossey 2013, xiv). Maybe many scientists have more channeling experiences than they realize. But because they do not believe, they don't see the experiences for what they are.

Perhaps you too have received some insight or creative thought that seemed to come out of nowhere. Often these ideas come through fully formed or in some symbolic way. You then need to translate or manifest them in some tangible way. This is a typical example of how art and science content is channeled.

Guidance and personal messages, ageless wisdom, descriptions of life in nonphysical realms, the past or the future, health and healing, information from or about deceased humans, artistic and creative expression and scientific discoveries—each of these can have a powerful impact on your life. There really is no limit to the type of information that you can receive through channeling.

Reflecting on your channeling experiences, write about the types of information you channeled. Do you notice any trends in the type of information that comes to you? If so, what type of information did you reveal? Was it only one specific type of information, or do you get information from different categories? If you don't feel you have had channeling experiences, think about the types of information you are most drawn to knowing.

You may have noticed in your reflection that the type of information you channel may depend on the channeling type your Noetic Signature highlights. I saw this in our and others' studies—that the type of information that channelers receive can be specialized. For example, remote viewers might be really good at knowing about distant locations, whereas someone else might be really good at knowing about the health of someone's body. You might have strong precognition about the future.

You can set an intention to learn more about what types of information your channeling aligns with most easily. You can also use your discernment to decide if the material you receive yourself or from others is relevant to your life and actionable.

Learning about these topics can inspire you to continue exploring channeling and its meaning in your own life. With practice, you can use your channeling to explore the areas that empower you and your life. In the next chapter, you will learn how to nurture your channeling in your own life.

CHAPTER 10

How to Channel Daily for Personal and Collective Good

There is no one right way to learn and develop your channeling. Channeling is always there and available to you. Developing your channeling is not about choosing the right method but learning how to open yourself to revealing or accessing it. Whatever path you take, I invite you to bring an attitude of patience and loving-kindness toward yourself in the process.

Channeling is often a yin or receptive, rather than a yang or directive, process. Multiple laboratory studies even show that when people "try" to channel, they don't do it as well. The most successful participants are relaxed. They are in a state of attentive awareness without a driven idea of how to do the task. They allow rather than try or force. If you find yourself with driven energy while channeling, take some nice deep breaths. Remind yourself of your intention and willingness. As best you can, surrender yourself to the process with love, kindness, and trust.

There are many ways to learn how to channel. You will learn key components for how to do that in this chapter if you feel comfortable embarking on learning how to channel on your own. You may want to channel in community with others or with a physical teacher guiding you. Many spiritual traditions have trainings that you can explore. Spiritualist practices around the world include channeling as a critical component. Most indigenous and shamanistic traditions also include aspects of channeling. Many books on how to channel are available to you, like *Opening to Channel* (Roman and Packer 1989). Psychic institutes in many metropolitan areas worldwide are too. You can also take online courses. I can't speak to the integrity and quality of these trainings, but I can say that the opportunities are there.

Use your intuition to see which path is best for you at this moment. That path might change for you over time. Trust your intuition, the insight you receive, and follow it. You'll find that you will likely feel like you are banging your head against a wall getting nowhere when it is the wrong way. When you are on the right path for you at that moment, it will feel easeful, as if the Universe is rising to support you.

Everyone's path to channeling is unique (Hastings 1991, 139; Hunter and Luke 2014; Emmons 2001; Emmons and Emmons 2003). Yours will be too. Where are you on your channeling path? Have you ever channeled before? You might be wondering how to channel. Have you already channeled? You may want to strengthen your skills or explore different channeling types.

All of the different channeling types are possible with your awareness, intention, and support. No matter where you are on your path, the following information will bring you insight and practical tips to discover or strengthen your channeling. First, I invite you, wherever you are, to allow the process to unfold. Everyone is different, and there is no one right way to channel. Trust your intuition in terms of the order and execution. In this chapter, I share the most commonly used elements for channeling.

Setting Up Your Body, Mind, and Environment

Preparing your body, mind, and space is a critical step on your channeling path. Preparation in each of these areas will support your clear channeling. Channeling in a chaotic place with a toxic body and cluttered mind makes channeling more challenging because the instrument you are using is taxed or strained.

Empowering Your Body

Empowering your body includes being aware of what you put into your body and how you move it. I invite you to become aware of your body's milieu if you are not already. What do you eat and drink? What products do you put on your body? Is your body tolerating electronic device exposure, such as from the amount of time you use your phone and computer? Are these empowering your body to function optimally?

Use your intuition to be impeccable with what you put into your body. Apply the discerning method I described in chapter 9 to learn about each of these things. For example, ask your body what it needs to nourish it most appropriately before eating or drinking. Expect that you will get an answer. Be still and listen. What is your body telling you?

You may find that the answers you receive about what your body needs change day by day and over time. Sometimes your body needs more protein. Sometimes your body needs electrolytes and minerals, which channeling can deplete. You may also notice that your body needs more water when you channel more often. Sometimes you need more nature time with movement. Sometimes you may need to be still and silent. You can do this discernment process for anything you put in or on your body and for how you move your body. It might feel strange to do this at first, but you'll find that it becomes second nature with practice.

You might notice that when you channel, you don't feel so great the next day. You might feel tired, be sore, or have other unusual physical or mental symptoms. Feeling lousy the next day doesn't mean that channeling hurt you. Usually, these symptoms are channeling revealing "stuff" you can clear. Channeling can act as a detoxifier. If you experience this, you can support your detoxification pathways. Rest. Drink lots of water. Take an Epsom salt bath. Take more minerals and eat nutrient-rich foods. Gentle movement, stretching, or yoga can support your body. Ask your body what it needs.

All these steps to empower your body will strengthen your channeling and your life in general.

Clearing Your Mind

Greater clarity of mind will support your easeful channeling. Being impeccable with your thinking is essential. Observe your thoughts. Notice what your mind is thinking. Are your thoughts positive and supportive of you? Or are they judgmental, critical, or ruminating on difficult or stressful situations? Do your thoughts dwell on negativity, or are they fearful of potential adverse future scenarios?

Imagine your thoughts as clouds moving across the sky of your awareness. You'll notice that you sometimes might not have many clouds, whereas on other days, the clouds are dark, gray, and covering the sky. Despite what the clouds look like, your awareness is ever present. Practice being aware of your thoughts and choosing thoughts that support you.

Meditation training is an excellent way to become aware of your thought process. Numerous meditation programs exist, from smartphone apps to in-person retreats. If you don't have a meditation practice already, I highly recommend that you start one. Being a meditator is one of the strongest predictors of channeling skill and experiences.

Personal growth work will also still your mind. Any process that clears egoic layers will dramatically strengthen your channeling. Your old woundings and unhealthy patterns learned from childhood, whether you are conscious of them or not, can block you from fully realizing your channeling potential. Clearing egoic layers will create easier channeling for you.

There are many methods to do this, like body-centered therapies, hypnotherapy, psychosynthesis, or psychotherapy. I use the simple yet profound methods for cleaning the ego from Leslie Temple-Thurston of CoreLight. The way these methods are described in *Returning to Oneness: The Seven Keys of Ascension*, I believe, are the most accessible for beginners.

If you don't have a process that you currently use, research different methods that attract you and use your intuition to choose which one is best for you. We all have egoic programming. You can channel more easily when you realize that your true essence is not your ego, and that your ego is part of you but not your whole self. With this perspective, you don't let ego get in the way. Through personal growth processes, you can view your egoic self with love and compassion and witness it transforming and expanding to hold your "bigger" self. This work can be intense but is well worth it.

Harmonizing Your Environment

Become discerning and meticulous about the space where you exist. Harmonizing your environment includes noticing what it is like in general and also creating your channeling space. Is your home chaotic, cluttered, or affected by difficult or unhealthy relationships? Take small steps with things you have control over to create harmony and balance in your personal space. For example, some parts of your home may be messy or cluttered. Look at each area as if you've never seen it before. See if there are things that you can release. Perhaps you can move furniture around to create a more flowing space. Consider adding art, plants, or other items that inspire you and bring you joy. There are excellent resources about creating harmony in your home, like *Clear Your Clutter with Feng Shui: Free Yourself from Physical, Mental, Emotional, and Spiritual Clutter Forever* by Karen Kingston and *The Life-Changing Magic of Tidying Up* by Marie Kondo.

For the things you don't have direct control over, lovingly envision a more optimal scenario. We all have something we don't have control over in our lives that we would like to be different. All we can do is focus on and make changes to what we do have control over. Ask for guidance on what you can do to transform what needs transforming and see what unfolds. You may find that difficult situations often resolve themselves in time or a solution you hadn't thought up arises when you focus on and empower yourself with channeling.

The second aspect of harmonizing your environment is to ready your channeling space. Where will you channel? There is no need for an extravagant setting. A quiet, peaceful place where you will not be disturbed is ideal. Gather any tools you like to use for channeling. Some people use items to help focus their attention and intention. These tools are not necessary, but some people find them helpful. These items include pendulums, crystals, tarot or divination cards, runes, and so forth. Bring yourself and your tools to your chosen channeling spot.

The next step is to clear yourself, your tools, and your environment. You can do this in many ways. You can simply mentally say, "I clear myself and this space of any energies that do not support my channeling session," with focused intention and will. You can burn incense or herbs, like sage, sweetgrass, or palo santo, which indigenous cultures have sacredly used in spiritual ceremonies for millennia for clearing and protection. Spritzing the area with an essential oil spray or lighting a candle also works. Sounds will also clear you and your space. Try using crystal or metal singing bowls or chimes. You can have fun exploring which clearing methods you like the best.

Clearing your body, mind, and environment will go a long way in creating an easeful channeling experience. Get into any comfortable position that works for you in your beautifully prepared channeling space. Most people find that a sitting meditation posture is most conducive to channeling. You and your channeling space are ready!

Clearly Stating Your Intention

In chapter 9, you learned that setting an intention entails directing your undivided attention and your will toward a specific outcome. Set intentions for your channeling on two levels: general and session-specific. General intentions are overarching desires for all your channeling. These intentions guide your channeling path and may not change very often. Here are some examples:

- You are safe and protected.

- Any obstacles blocking your clear and direct channel are removed.

- You are willing to learn new things, change, and expand.

- Your channeling benefits you, those around you, and humanity.

Setting intentions around your attitude toward channeling can also be helpful. Your attitude of willingness, openness, patience, trust that you can channel, and loving-kindness toward yourself during the process will support frustration-free channeling.

Declare your overall channeling development intentions. For example, you may want to strengthen the channeling type you've experienced. Suppose you hear an inner voice, but not as clearly or as often as you would like. A general intention could be that your inner-voice channeling becomes more precise and louder. Set the intention that you will effortlessly discern between your mental processes and a channeled inner voice.

You have your unique Noetic Signature. You naturally align with specific types of channeling more than others. For example, you may want to use your mind to affect physical things. Yet, not all people are equally adept at psychokinesis. You may learn how to move objects with diligent practice to a certain degree successfully. However, the learning process may be more difficult for you than someone whose Noetic Signature is more robust in psychokinesis. You can use your intention to declare which channeling type you want to strengthen and clarify with practice.

Examine your motivations to channel to clarify your general intentions and improve your channeling. Be aware of what motivates you. Channeling growth is not stimulated by selfish or self-serving goals. The desire to use channeling for material gain or other harmful outcomes is unproductive.

Interestingly, most professional channelers I know receive their needed financial support more quickly when they don't focus on making money.

After declaring your general intentions, think about your session-specific intentions. Specific intentions are your desires for each session and will change session to session. What is the purpose and intention of this session? Do you have a particular question or information you want to know? Is there a specific energy type you wish to channel, such as energy for healing? Is the session for you or someone else? Declare the outcomes you want to see for this session. You may also choose to write these intentions down or speak them into a voice recorder.

Setting your general and specific intentions consciously and mindfully creates a symbolic container to hold you on your channeling path.

Invoking Grounding and Protection

Grounding and protection are the next steps to take after setting your general and specific intentions. Sometimes people feel disembodied or "floaty" when they first channel, meditate, or experience other altered states of consciousness. This ungrounded feeling can be uncomfortable or cause anxiety. You can ground yourself before your channeling to help avoid this. Grounding can happen in many ways. You can simply say with focus and will, "I ground myself now." You can also visualize yourself grounded to the earth. Imagine a tether going from your root chakra, between your anus and perineum, through Earth's layers and anchoring to the center's iron crystal. Other visualizations include:

- imagining your bare feet touching the earth,

- seeing your legs expanding and being heavy on the earth, and

- growing tree roots that extend into the earth.

Explore grounding techniques that support you. When you feel connected to the earth, you will feel grounded while channeling (or at any time, for that matter).

Protecting yourself is another essential aspect of channeling. In general, there is nothing to fear, and no harm will come to you during your channeling sessions. However, protecting yourself may prevent unnecessary side effects some experience when channeling. You may have already experienced being very open to energy or information that overwhelmed your nervous system and even caused adverse physical effects. It is true that we are all one and interconnected. There is nothing wrong or separate about the different energies that you sense. However, being very open to energy that does not resonate with you can affect your energetic state, physical body, and mental well-being. Preventing overwhelm and protecting yourself in general and when channeling are imperative. Always protect yourself before going into an energetically intense situation, any channeling session, and even when you leave home for the day.

As an empath, I do this before going into large crowds. Otherwise, I can feel overwhelmed by other people's emotions. I don't protect myself because emotions are evil or out to get me. My protection supports my nervous system, and I do it because I know that I am sensitive to other people's feelings. Invoking protection is just like putting on a raincoat and bringing an umbrella when it is pouring rain outside. Invoking protection is a way to care for yourself.

There are many methods to protect yourself energetically and physically. The simplest is with intention. You can declare your intention by saying, "I am safe and protected." Visualizations work very well for protection also. One of my favorites is to visualize an impenetrable bubble around me, sometimes golden white, sometimes a beautiful blue, that blocks energy not aligned with me. Another fun visualization is to imagine putting on a large bodysuit and zipping it up to protect you. Children love these exercises. Get creative exploring what protection techniques work best for you.

Calling on Helpers

Developing a relationship with your nonphysical helper team can support your protection process and your channeling. My personal experiences have led me to believe that nonphysical beings help me on my channeling journey. This concept may or may not resonate with you. If it does, please read on. You can still channel if it doesn't; please skip this section.

Connecting with your nonphysical support team, what many people call guides or spiritual guides, can boost your protection while developing your channeling abilities. Here is what I have come to understand about guide relationships through my firsthand experiences and study. Each human is assigned a nonphysical multidimensional being to support them on their path. All humans have free will and can freely choose their actions. However, before incarnating into this body, you, along with your guidance team, created a plan for your life's mission, how you imagined your life would unfold.

Your guides align with you on this plan. They support you to fulfill what you chose before your incarnation. You may have more than one. Spiritualist traditions believe that mediums are born with a minimum of five spirit guides (Emmons and Emmons 2003, 238). One guide may be the primary spokesperson, if you will, of your team. Each guide on your team may support you in different ways. Your guides may take various forms. In shamanic traditions, power animals act as guides. Your guides may also change over your lifetime.

Developing a healthy, collaborative relationship with this team will accelerate your channeling development. Your guides are powerful agents who can help ensure your safety and protection during channeling. Your guides are available to you at all times. You can include an intention to connect with your guides as part of your intention-setting process. Ask that they present themselves to you in a way that you can perceive. Ask to strengthen your relationship with them. I have never had anyone who seriously asked to communicate with their guides not receive an answer. Once you establish a connection, you can include calling on your guides as part of your invoking-protection process during your day and for channeling. Know that your relationship with your guides will flourish by bringing your heartfelt intention for collaboration and support.

Revealing Information and Energy

At this point, you might feel like there are a lot of steps to channeling. I understand, and you are not alone. I know that it can feel overwhelming at first. With practice, you'll find that you can move through these steps quite quickly. After these steps, the "channeling" part of channeling is quite simple.

While in your channeling position, take some deep breaths. Feel your mind and body completely relaxed.

Open yourself to channeling. You are receptive and still. Be in a state of willingness and allowing. You hold the truth that you are more than your physical body and that your consciousness expands beyond it. Ask your question. Then wait. Trust what you receive, whether it is visual, a sound or voice, or sensations in your body. If you are unclear, ask to perceive the information again differently or more clearly. Trust that whatever you received is what you needed at the moment, even if you think you didn't receive anything.

You may find that waiting in a receptive state is uncomfortable. You can try using visualizations to support your process. I sometimes use a chakra meditation to initiate a receptive state. I envision each chakra, from root to crown. I imagine myself suspended between heaven and Earth. Grounded to Earth and open to the wisdom of the Cosmos, my body is a channel available to receive information and energy. Remember that there is no trying or forcing in channeling.

Your attitude of loving-kindness, patience, and trust in this process will support you to progress with ease and flow. If you find yourself frustrated while receiving, remember that there is no right or wrong channeling method. Try something different. Most importantly, try again. You will find a way to channel that is your way.

Closing Your Session

Formal sessions last anywhere from a few minutes to a couple of hours, depending on your questions and experience level. Continue your channeling until you feel your session is complete. You can then formally close the session. Closing includes closing your channel, an offering of gratitude, and declaring the session closed. You can close your session in a way that is meaningful to you.

Closing your channel is a crucial step. You can close your channel by saying with intention, "I close my channel now." You can also visualize an image or symbol that you connect with closing your channel. For example, my crown chakra is wide open when I channel. The aperture of a camera is the part that opens and closes to let the light come in. I imagine my crown chakra closing like a camera shutter to a smaller aperture when I stop channeling.

Closing your channel in this way prevents your nervous or other systems from being overwhelmed. When you channel, aspects of yourself are likely very open, making it difficult to function normally in your everyday life.

Suppose you move through your typical day with your channeling abilities wide open. In that case, the amount of information that comes in can tax your nervous system.

I have counseled people who had an abrupt awakening into channeling. You may have heard stories about this as well. Receiving an onslaught of information and energy through channeling when you are not quite ready for it is overwhelming and scary. Taking substances that induce an altered state of consciousness can remove the obstacles to your channeling abilities too quickly. You may suddenly access too much information and energy without your usual filters. Taking substances may be the right path for some people, in the right context, and with the proper support.

Regardless of how you get into the channeling state, closing your channel is necessary. You can then offer gratitude for your inherent channeling capacity, your specific channeling abilities, and all that supports you in it. Thank anyone or anything that you feel needs thanking.

The final step is to declare the session complete. You can symbolize the session's completion by ringing a bell or chime or some other way that inspires you.

Use these steps as an outline, a skeleton structure, to create your unique channeling process.

1. Empower your body.

2. Clear your mind.

3. Harmonize your environment.

4. Clearly state your general and specific intentions.

5. Invoke grounding and protection.

6. Call on helpers.

7. Reveal information and energy.

8. Close your session.

Be open and curious about what works and doesn't work for you. Have fun! Channeling can bring much joy and lightheartedness into your life.

Bringing Channeling into Everyday Life

You just learned about common elements of an intentional channeling session. However, you might have channeling experiences spontaneously, whether you want them or not. Formal channeling practice does not prevent spontaneous experiences happening in your daily life.

One simple channeling practice you can do beyond formal sessions is to dream channel. Ask a specific question you'd like to answer. Set the intention that you will receive an answer, and then go to sleep and dream. In the morning, write your dreams down. Notice if any symbols, information, or situations were relevant to your question.

You can also "tune in" at any time, for any reason, about anything. You can receive insight into which way to go while driving, what to choose while shopping, or guidance for parenting or relationship issues outside of formal sessions. Information through our interconnected Universe is always available to you.

You learned how to close your channel to prevent being overwhelmed in the last section. What is the balance between being wide open, making normal daily functions difficult, and completely closed, blocking your intuition or spontaneous insights? Imagine the camera aperture metaphor. During channeling sessions, your aperture could be 100 percent open. For your everyday activities, you could leave it 20 percent open. Going into a large crowd, you could close it completely. Explore the appropriate percentages that work for you to be highly functioning in different situations. You will notice that this percentage shifts and changes throughout your day.

Bringing your awareness to this will help you receive the most benefit from your channeling abilities. It can also enable you to deal with stress and manage your energy. Successfully managing my channel openness has dramatically improved my health. When I find myself run-down or stressed, I'm often not using the tools I just described. We will not remember to use these tools all the time—and these are excellent opportunities for you to practice your attitude of loving-kindness, patience, and compassion.

Channeling practice is something you repeat over and over again— ideally, daily. Whatever methods you use, eventually you'll likely find that channeling becomes second nature. You will naturally have moments of stillness to resource what you need to know for the best way forward in your day. Soon, positive results will arise that inspire and motivate you to continue.

Why Channel?

Channeling can be good for you. In earlier chapters, you saw that when researchers measure the impact of channeling in various people, the results are, on average, overwhelmingly positive. People who channel are high functioning and have greater levels of well-being. People feel positively impacted by their experiences. They also find value and meaning in them.

Channeling has protected people from dangerous situations. Channeling provides comfort and a sense of security. People's self-awareness, introspection, and understanding of themselves have improved from channeling. Channeling also helps people make decisions. Making decisions was one of the most noted uses of channeling in our studies. People use channeling as a resource. A resource more inclusive than their logic and rational mind. More expanded than their traditional five senses. In general, people also find that when they follow channeled insights for decision making, their lives are more easeful.

Channeling also offers a way to be of service to our communities and humanity. Rather than directing your sessions for personal questions or healing, you can help others. During your sessions, ask yourself, "What can I do right now to support the collective evolution of humanity with my channeling?" Then wait for the answer. Sometimes the solution is to sit in meditation while envisioning a positive future on a specific challenging world issue. For example, a group of channelers and scientists currently collaborate on global warming and environmental pollution solutions. Others are intending and envisioning a positive future world. Others use "seeing" to discover the genetic components at play in psychic abilities. There is an infinite number of ways to use your channeling skills to support yourself and others. What issue on our planet breaks your heart the most? Bring your channeling practice to transforming that issue. Trust your insight on the topic. Trust your guidance on the next most appropriate step for you to take to manifest positive transformation.

Conclusion

Our world needs us. Our world agonizes from war, violence, and suffering on all levels. It often appears as if our world seems to be in chaos and that chaos will never change—that we will never see the more harmonious and peaceful world many of us yearn to know. You can use your clearing, protection, intention, willingness, and expanding to support not just the personal self but also those around you and humanity, and to make a difference. Your practice adds to all the love, beauty, community, and hope our world also knows. Humanity *is* evolving. Your channeling accelerates that evolution.

Here is a metaphor for what is happening on the planet right now. Imagine a glass filled with clear water. The glass looks clear except for a layer of mud at the bottom of the glass. You could say that only the surface water is clear. When pure, clear water pours into the glass, the mud at the bottom stirs up. The water now appears muddy. Humanity is like this glass of water. The world seems to be very muddy and dirty. Yet, as more clear water pours into the glass—as each of us, individual by individual, acknowledges our true nature—the water gets clearer. You will come to understand that:

- your consciousness is not limited to your physical brain and body,

- your consciousness has no limits and can expand beyond your conventional notions of space and time,

- you have an infinite amount of resources available to you beyond our traditional five senses, and

- you are interconnected to all that is.

Through this process, the water will eventually become crystal clear with no mud at the bottom. Things will change. It is inevitable. Take heart. The positive, beautiful, collective, interconnected future you wish for yourself will become a reality in due time. Embracing your channeling capacity as your human birthright will magnificently support this effort. Nurturing and developing your channeling ability are potent ways to accelerate this change.

As you acknowledge, embrace, and use your channeling abilities, the effect will ripple out to those around you. People will ask you, "What are you doing? Teach me." You may feel some anxiety or nervousness about "coming out of the channeling closet." *What will people think of me? What will they say?* Throughout this book, you have seen the strong evidence that channeling is a real phenomenon, despite the skepticism, criticism, and taboos.

Release those worries as best you can. Know the direct experience within yourself. Trust that channeling is valid. It *will* support you in your life. I am deeply grateful for your willingness and your courage to have made it to the end of this book. I hope that it has provided you with a broad understanding of channeling science and given you a guiding light on your channeling path.

May this book impart what you need to continue your transformation, awakening your spirit, mind, and being to the nature of who you are and your true potential. Please know you are loved. You are supported. Together, we will manifest humanity's beautiful future.

Glossary of Channeling Terms

automatic writing, or psychography. A motor automatism in which a person's hand writes meaningful statements, but without the writer consciously premeditating the content of what is produced.

clairalience. Clear smelling; to smell a fragrance/odor of substance or food that is not in one's surroundings.

clairaudience. Clear audio/hearing; extrasensory data perceived as sound, generally considered a facet of clairvoyance.

claircognizance, or knowing. Clear knowing; having the ability to understand or know something without any direct evidence or reasoning process.

clairempathy. Clear emotion; to feel the emotions of another person or nonphysical entity (also known as an empath). This is different than "normal" empathy or compassion, but the literal feeling of another's emotions rather than just empathizing with them. Clairempathy can often include the ability to heal, transform, or transmute emotions as well.

clairgustance. Clear tasting; to taste without putting anything in one's mouth.

clairsentience. Clear sensation or feeling within the whole body without any outer stimuli related to the feeling or information; "just knowing" information that others can't access with their normal senses; extrasensory data perceived as heightened feeling or awareness. Generally considered a facet of clairvoyance. Sometimes also termed "telaesthesia."

clairtangency (also psychometry or psychoscopy). Clear touching; obtaining paranormal information about an object or its owner by holding it in one's hands.

clairvoyance. Clear vision; paranormal acquisition of information concerning an object or contemporary physical event. This is the broad definition of clairvoyance that would also incorporate many of the other "clairs" within it. Others use a more specific definition of clairvoyance referring to extrasensory data perceived visually. Remote viewing (the practice of seeking impressions about a distant or unseen target), aura reading (perception of energy fields surrounding people, places, and things), geomancy (perception of the energy of places and of the land, such as ley lines), nature empathy (extrasensory perception of information about and communicating with nature and plants), and animal communication (extrasensory perception of information about and communication with animals) could all be considered aspects of clairvoyance.

medium. One who communicates with discarnate or deceased personalities on a regular basis, or more generally, a person who perceives, communicates, and/or demonstrates ostensibly paranormal phenomena regularly and/or with some degree of ability to do so at will. A term less favored by psychical researchers than "sensitive" or "psychic" since "medium" implies a "go-between" and is used by spiritualists to indicate the person acting as a means of communicating with purported surviving discarnate personalities (Ashby 1987).

nonlocal aspects of consciousness. Near-death experiences (NDEs), out of body experiences (OBEs), and astral projection (or astral travel) are all experiences where the consciousness ostensibly extends beyond the confines of the body in some way. These events can be triggered spontaneously, as in near-death experiences or some out-of-body experiences, while some are initiated by those with the capacity to control it. OBEs and astral projection are likely different terms for the same experience. An out-of-body experience is one in which the "astral body" separates from the physical body and is capable of traveling outside it.

precognition/presentience, retrocognition/retrosentience. Precognition is a form of extrasensory perception in which the target is some future event that cannot be deduced from normally known data in the present. Precognition is considered by some a form of clairvoyance. Presentience is the same, but the information is usually sensed with the body rather than known through cognition (e.g., heart rate, pupil dilation, skin conductance). Premonition is the feeling or impression that something is about to happen, especially something ominous or dire, yet about which no normal information is available. Retrocognition or postcognition refers to a form of extrasensory perception in which the target is some past event that could not have been learned or inferred by normal means.

psychokinesis (PK), or telekinesis. Manipulation of objects/targets by the mind without the use of physical means. In macro-PK, the targets are larger than quantum-mechanical processes, such as microorganisms, dice, metal (spoons), and other macroscopic objects. Examples of this also include levitation, pyrokinesis (creating or manipulating fire), healing, transforming or transmuting physical bodies, and psychic surgery (removal of diseased body tissue without the use of anesthesia or surgical instruments, and/or when bleeding and infection are inhibited paranormally).

telepathy. The paranormal acquisition of information concerning the thoughts, feelings, or activity of another conscious being.

trance or full-trance mediumship or channeling. A form of channeling in which an individual willingly enters degrees of trancelike states of consciousness, whereby the channel connects with sources of information that appear to exist outside of their ego awareness.

Acknowledgments

The birthing of a book is a collaborative process. I could not have completed this without the incredible support of so many people. My gratitude begins with my family, who opened me up to my channeling experiences. I especially want to thank my mother Maha Kury, grandmother Hiyam Kury, and all the channelers in my family who have gone before me. I would also like to thank my grandfather Costa Kury for his trailblazing and commitment to channeling.

This book began with Matthew McKay, who heard me talking about the Science of Channeling program at IONS and said, "You should write a book about that." That led to a beautiful partnership with New Harbinger Publications. The entire New Harbinger team, including Ryan Buresh and Jennifer Holder, helped make my scientific idea and language into an accessible lay-language book. Thank you to Gretel Hakanson for her excellent copy editing.

Thank you to Claire Lachance, who spearheaded the collaboration with New Harbinger and provided personal and professional support, making it possible for me to focus on this project. I am grateful to the entire IONS science team who inspire and motivate me every day to keep going despite the obstacles, one deep breath at a time.

Last but not least, I am deeply thankful for my wonderful husband, who gave me the space to do what I needed to do, and for my sweet son Mateen, who brings so much joy into my life in intense and crazy times.

References

Achterberg, J., K. Cooke, T. Richards, L. J. Standish, and L. Kozak. 2005. "Evidence for Correlations Between Distant Intentionality and Brain Function in Recipients: A Functional Magnetic Resonance Imaging Analysis." *Journal of Alternative and Complementary Medicine* 11, no. 6: 965–971.

Alexander, E. 2012. *Proof of Heaven: A Neurosurgeon's Journey into the Afterlife.* New York: Simon & Schuster.

Alvarado, C. S. 2008. "Spontaneous Precognition: A Bibliographical Note." *Explore* 4, no. 5: 294.

American Psychiatric Association. 2013. *Diagnostic and Statistical Manual of Mental Disorders.* 5th ed. Washington DC: American Psychiatric Publishing, Inc.

Anastasia, J., A. Delorme, J. Okonsky, and H. Wahbeh. 2020. "A Qualitative Exploratory Analysis of Channeled Content." *Explore* 16, no. 4: 231–236. https://doi.org/10.1016/j.explore.2020.02.008

Armour, C., K. I. Karstoft, and J. D. Richardson. 2014. "The Co-Occurrence of PTSD and Dissociation: Differentiating Severe PTSD from Dissociative-PTSD." *Social Psychiatry and Psychiatric Epidemiology* 49, no. 8: 1297–1306. https://doi.org/10.1007/s00127-014-0819-y

Aron, E. N., and A. Aron. 1997. "Sensory-Processing Sensitivity and Its Relation to Introversion and Emotionality." *Journal of Personality and Social Psychology* 73, no. 2: 345–368.

Ashby, R. H. 1987. *The Ashby Guidebook for Study of the Paranormal.* Published in collaboration with Spiritual Frontiers Fellowship by S. Weiser.

Assagioli, R. 1965. *Psychosynthesis.* New York: Hobbs, Dorman & Company.

Bacon, F. 1670. *Sylva Sylvarum, or a Natural History in Ten Centuries.* JR.

Bader, C. D., F. C. Mencken, and J. O. Baker. 2017. *Paranormal America: Ghost Encounters, UFO Sightings, Bigfoot Hunts, and Other Curiosities in Religion and Culture.* New York: NYU Press.

Bancel, P. A. 2017. "Searching for Global Consciousness: A 17-Year Exploration." *Explore* 13, no. 2: 94–101.

Baptista, J., M. Derakhshani, and P. E. Tressoldi. 2015. "Explicit Anomalous Cognition: A Review of the Best Evidence in Ganzfeld, Forced Choice, Remote Viewing and Dream Studies." In *Parapsychology: A Handbook for the 21st Century,* edited by E. Cardeña, J. Palmer, and D. Marcusson-Clavertz, 192–214. Jefferson, NC: McFarland & Company.

Barker, S. A. 2018. "N, N-Dimethyltryptamine (DMT), an Endogenous Hallucinogen: Past, Present, and Future Research to Determine Its Role and Function." *Frontiers in Neuroscience* 12 (August). https://doi.org/10.3389/fnins.2018.00536

Bastos, M. A. V., Jr., P. R. H. O. Bastos, M. L. dos Santos, D. Iandoli, Jr., R. B. Portella, and G. Lucchetti. 2018. "Comparing the Detection of Endogenous Psychedelics in Individuals with and without Alleged Mediumistic Experiences." *Explore* 14, no. 6: 448–452.

Bastos, M. A. V., P. R. H. O. Bastos, L. M. Goncalves, I. H. S. Osório, and G. Lucchetti. 2015. "Mediumship: Review of Quantitative Studies Published in the 21st Century." *Archives of Clinical Psychiatry* 42, no. 5: 129–138.

Bastos, M. A. V., P. R. H. O. Bastos, I. H. S. Osório, K. A. R. C. Muass, D. Iandoli Jr., and G. Lucchetti. 2016. "Frontal Electroencephalographic (EEG) Activity and Mediumship: A Comparative Study Between Spiritist Mediums and Controls." *Archives of Clinical Psychiatry (São Paulo)* 43, no. 2: 20–26. https://doi.org/10.1590/0101-60830000000076

Bastos, M. A. V., Jr., P. R. H. O. Bastos, I. H. S. Osório, S. A. M. Pinheiro, D. Iandoli, Jr., and G. Lucchetti. 2018. "Physiologic Correlates of Culture-Bound Dissociation: A Comparative Study of Brazilian Spiritist Mediums and Controls." *Transcultural Psychiatry* 55, no. 2: 286–313.

Behling, O., and H. Eckel. 1991. "Making Sense out of Intuition." *Academy of Management Executive* 5, no. 1: 46–54.

Beischel, J. 2014. "Assisted After-Death Communication: A Self-Prescribed Treatment for Grief." *Journal of Near-Death Studies* 32: 161–165.

———. 2019. "Spontaneous, Facilitated, Assisted, and Requested After-Death Communication Experiences and Their Impact on Grief." *Threshold: Journal of Interdisciplinary Consciousness Studies* 3, no. 1: 1–32.

Beischel, J., M. Boccuzzi, M. Biuso, and A. J. Rock. 2015. "Anomalous Information Reception by Research Mediums Under Blinded Conditions II: Replication and Extension." *Explore* 11, no. 2: 136–142. https://doi.org/10.1016/j.explore.2015.01.001

Beischel, J., C. Mosher, and M. Boccuzzi. 2015. "The Possible Effects on Bereavement of Assisted After-Death Communication During Readings with Psychic Mediums: A Continuing Bonds Perspective." *Omega: Journal of Death and Dying* 70, no. 2: 169–194. https://doi.org/10.2190/OM.70.2.b

———. 2017. "Quantitative and Qualitative Analyses of Mediumistic and Psychic Experiences." *Threshold: Journal of Interdisciplinary Consciousness Studies* 1, no. 2: 51–91.

Beischel, J., and A. J. Rock. 2009. "Addressing the Survival Versus Psi Debate through Process-Focused Mediumship Research." *The Journal of Parapsychology* 73: 71.

Beischel, J., and G. E. Schwartz. 2007. "Anomalous Information Reception by Research Mediums Demonstrated Using a Novel Triple-Blind Protocol." *Explore* 3, no. 1: 23–27. https://doi.org/10.1016/j.explore.2006.10.004

Beischel, J., S. Tassone, and M. Boccuzzi. 2019. "Hematological and Psychophysiological Correlates of Anomalous Information Reception in Mediums: A Preliminary Exploration." *Explore* 15, no. 2: 126–133. https://doi.org/10.1016/j.explore.2018 .04.009

Beischel, J., and N. L. Zingrone. 2015. "Mental Mediumship." In *Parapsychology: A Handbook for the 21st Century*, edited by E. Cardeña, J. Palmer, and D. Marcusson-Clavertz, 301–313. Jefferson, NC: McFarland & Company.

Beloff, J., and L. Evans. 1961. "A Radioactivity Test of Psycho-Kinesis." *Journal of the Society for Psychical Research* 41: 41–46.

Bem, D. J. 1993. "The Ganzfeld Experiment." *The Journal of Parapsychology* 57, no. 2: 101–111.

———. 2011. "Feeling the Future: Experimental Evidence for Anomalous Retroactive Influences on Cognition and Affect." *Journal of Personality and Social Psychology* 100, no. 3: 407–425.

Bem, D. J., and C. Honorton. 1994. "Does Psi Exist? Replicable Evidence for an Anomalous Process of Information Transfer." *Psychological Bulletin* 115, no. 1: 4.

Bem, D. J., J. Palmer, and R. S. Broughton. 2001. "Updating the Ganzfeld Database: A Victim of Its Own Success?" *Journal of Parapsychology* 65: 207–218.

Bem, D. J., P. Tressoldi, T. Rabeyron, and M. Duggan. 2016. "Feeling the Future: A Meta-Analysis of 90 Experiments on the Anomalous Anticipation of Random Future Events." *F1000Research* 4: 1188. https://doi.org/10.12688/f1000research .7177.2

Benfey, O. T. 1958. "August Kekulé and the Birth of the Structural Theory of Organic Chemistry in 1858." *Journal of Chemical Education* 35, no. 1: 21.

Bierman, D. J., and T. Rabeyron. 2013. "Can Psi Research Sponsor Itself? Simulations and Results of an Automated ARV-Casino Experiment."

Bierman, D. J., J. P. Spottiswoode, and A. Bijl. 2016. "Testing for Questionable Research Practices in a Meta-Analysis: An Example from Experimental Parapsychology." *PloS One* 11, no. 5: e0153049. https://doi.org/10.1371/journal.pone.0153049

Blake, W. 1803. "Letter to Thomas Butts, 25 April 1803." The William Blake Archive. 1803. http://www.blakearchive.org/copy/letters?descId=lt25april1803.1.ltr.03

Born, M. 1971. *The Born Einstein Letters*. New York: Macmilllan Press LTD. http:// archive.org/details/TheBornEinsteinLetters

Bosch, H., F. Steinkamp, and E. Boller. 2006. "Examining Psychokinesis: The Interaction of Human Intention with Random Number Generators— a Meta-Analysis." *Psychological Bulletin* 132, no. 4: 497–523.

Bouchard, T. J., M. McGue, D. Lykken, and A. Tellegen. 1999. "Intrinsic and Extrinsic Religiousness: Genetic and Environmental Influences and Personality Correlates." *Twin Research and Human Genetics* 2, no. 2: 88–98.

Bourguignon, E. 1973. *Religion, Altered States of Consciousness, and Social Change.* Columbus, OH: The Ohio State University Press.

————. 1976. *Possession.* San Francisco: Chandler & Sharp Publishers.

Bragazzi, N. L., H. Khabbache, M. Perduca, B. Neri, F. Firenzuoli, G. Penazzi, M. Simões, R. Zerbetto, and T. Simona Re. 2018. "Parapsychology, N, N-Dimethyltryptamine, and the Pineal Gland." *Cosmos and History: The Journal of Natural and Social Philosophy* 14, no. 2: 228–238.

Braud, W. G., R. Wood, and L. W. Braud. 1975. "Free-Response GESP Performance During an Experimental Hypnagogic State Induced by Visual and Acoustic Ganzfeld Techniques: A Replication and Extension." *Journal of the American Society for Psychical Research* 69, no. 2: 105–113.

Braude, S. E. 2003. *Immortal Remains: The Evidence for Life After Death.* Lanham, MD: Rowman & Littlefield Publishing Group.

Braude, S. E. 2015. "Macro-Psychokinesis." In *Parapsychology: A Handbook for the 21st Century,* edited by E. Cardeña, J. Palmer, and D. Marcusson-Clavertz, 258–265. Jefferson, NC: McFarland & Company.

Bub, J. 2019. "Quantum Entanglement and Information." In *The Stanford Encyclopedia of Philosophy,* edited by E. N. Zalta. Stanford, CA: Metaphysics Research Lab, Stanford University. https://plato.stanford.edu/archives/spr2019/entries/qt-entangle/

Buniy, R. V., and S. D. H. Hsu. 2012. "Everything Is Entangled." *Physics Letters B* 718, no. 2: 233–236. https://doi.org/10.1016/j.physletb.2012.09.047

Burkert, W. 1991. *Greek Religion.* New York: Wiley-Blackwell, Harvard Press.

Cahn, R., and J. Polich. 2006. "Meditation States and Traits: EEG, ERP, and Neuroimaging Studies." *Psychological Bulletin* 132: 180–211.

Capra, C., D. J. Kavanagh, L. Hides, and J. G. Scott. 2015. "Current CAPE-15: A Measure of Recent Psychotic-like Experiences and Associated Distress." *Early Intervention in Psychiatry* (May). https://doi.org/10.1111/eip.12245

Cardeña, E. 2014. "A Call for an Open, Informed Study of All Aspects of Consciousness." *Frontiers in Human Neuroscience* 8, no. 17. https://doi.org/10.3389/fnhum.2014.00017

————. 2015. "The Unbearable Fear of Psi: On Scientific Suppression in the 21st Century." *Journal of Scientific Exploration* 29, no. 4: 601–620.

————. 2018. "The Experimental Evidence for Parapsychological Phenomena: A Review." *American Psychologist* 73, no. 5: 663–677. https://doi.org/10.1037/amp0000236

Cardeña, E., and D. Marcusson-Clavertz. 2015. "States, Traits, Cognitive Variables, and Psi." In *Parapsychology: A Handbook for the 21st Century,* edited by E. Cardeña, J. Palmer, and D. Marcusson-Clavertz, 110–124. Jefferson, NC: McFarland & Company.

Cardeña, E., J. Palmer, and D. Marcusson-Clavertz. 2015. *Parapsychology: A Handbook for the 21st Century.* Jefferson, NC: McFarland & Company.

Cardeña, E., M. van Duijl, L. Weiner, and D. Terhune. 2009. "Possession/Trance Phenomena." *Dissociation and the Dissociative Disorders: DSM-V and Beyond,* 171–181.

Carhart-Harris, R. L., D. Erritzoe, T. Williams, J. M. Stone, L. J. Reed, A. Colasanti, R. J. Tyacke, et al. 2012. "Neural Correlates of the Psychedelic State as Determined by fMRI Studies with Psilocybin." *Proceedings of the National Academy of Sciences* 109, no. 6: 2138–2143. https://doi.org/10.1073/pnas.1119598109

Carpenter, J. n.d. "First Sight: A Model and a Theory of Psi." http://carpenterpsychology.com/. http://carpenterpsychology.com/about/documents/FirstSightformindfield.pdf

Castillo, R. J. 2003. "Trance, Functional Psychosis, and Culture." *Psychiatry: Interpersonal and Biological Processes* 66, no. 1: 9–21.

Castro, M., R. Burrows, and R. Wooffitt. 2014a. "The Paranormal Is (Still) Normal: The Sociological Implications of a Survey of Paranormal Experiences in Great Britain." *Sociological Research Online* 19, no. 3: 16.

———. 2014b. "The Paranormal Is (Still) Normal: The Sociological Implications of a Survey of Paranormal Experiences in Great Britain." *Sociological Research Online* 19, no. 3: 16.

Celenza, C. S. 2017. "Marsilio Ficino." In *The Stanford Encyclopedia of Philosophy,* edited by E. N. Zalta (Fall). Stanford, CA: Metaphysics Research Lab, Stanford University. https://plato.stanford.edu/archives/fall2017/entries/ficino/

Chalmers, D. J. 1996. *The Conscious Mind: In Search of a Fundamental Theory.* Philosophy of Mind Series. New York: Oxford University Press.

Claridge, G. E. 1997. *Schizotypy: Implications for Illness and Health.* London: Oxford University Press.

Cohn, S. A. 1994. "A Survey on Scottish Second Sight." *Journal of the Society for Psychical Research* 59, no. 835: 385–400.

———. 1999. "Second Sight and Family History: Pedigree and Segregation Analyses." *Journal of Scientific Exploration* 13, no. 3: 351–372.

Cook, G. 2020. "Does Consciousness Pervade the Universe?" *Scientific American.* (January 14). https://www.scientificamerican.com/article/does-consciousness-pervade-the-universe/

Coons, P. M. 1994. "Confirmation of Childhood Abuse in Child and Adolescent Cases of Multiple Personality Disorder and Dissociative Disorder Not Otherwise Specified." *The Journal of Nervous and Mental Disease* 182, no. 8: 461–464.

Crook, J. H. 1997. "The Indigenous Psychiatry of Ladakh, Part I: Practice Theory Approaches to Trance Possession in the Himalayas." *Anthropology & Medicine* 4, no. 3: 289–307. https://doi.org/10.1080/13648470.1997.9964539

Currivan, J. 2017. *The Cosmic Hologram: In-Formation at the Center of Creation.* New York: Simon & Schuster.

de Waal, F. B. M., and S. D. Preston. 2017. "Mammalian Empathy: Behavioural Manifestations and Neural Basis." *Nature Review Neuroscience* 18, no. 8: 498–509. https://doi.org/10.1038/nrn.2017.72

Dein, S. 2012. "Mental Health and the Paranormal." *Mental Health* 1: 1–2012.

Delorme, A. 2013. "Matthieu Ricard Telling the Story of a Telepathy Experience with His Teacher." Accessed May 3, 2020. https://www.youtube.com/watch?v=4sgDtju8F4A

Delorme, A., J. Beischel, L. Michel, M. Boccuzzi, D. Radin, and P. J. Mills. 2013. "Electrocortical Activity Associated with Subjective Communication with the Deceased." *Frontiers in Psychology* 4. https://doi.org/10.3389/fpsyg.2013.00834

Delorme, A., A. Pierce, L. Michel, and D. Radin. 2018. "Intuitive Assessment of Mortality Based on Facial Characteristics: Behavioral, Electrocortical, and Machine Learning Analyses." *Explore* 14, no. 4: 262–267. https://doi.org/10.1016/j.explore.2017.10.011

Delorme, A., Cannard, C., Radin, D., and Wahbeh, H. 2020. "Accuracy and neural correlates of blinded mediumship compared to controls on an image classification task." *Brain and Cognition*, 146, 105638. https://doi.org/10.1016/j.bandc.2020.105638

Don, N. S., and G. Moura. 2000. "Trance Surgery in Brazil." *Alternative Therapies in Health and Medicine* 6, no. 4: 39–48.

Dossey, L. 2009. *The Power of Premonitions.* New York: Dutton Adult.

———. 2013. *One Mind: How Our Individual Mind Is Part of a Great Consciousness and Why It Matters.* Carlsbad, CA: Hay House.

Dunne, B. J., and R. G. Jahn. 1992. "Experiments in Remote Human/Machine Interaction." *Journal of Scientific Exploration* 6, no. 4: 311.

Dunne, B. J., and R. G. Jahn. 2003. "Information and Uncertainty in Remote Perception Research." *Journal of Scientific Exploration* 17, no. 2: 207–241.

Ellison, C. G., and D. Fan. 2008. "Daily Spiritual Experiences and Psychological Well-Being Among US Adults." *Social Indicators Research* 88, no. 2: 247–271.

Emmons, C. F. 2001. "On Becoming a Spirit Medium in a 'Rational Society.'" *Anthropology of Consciousness* 12, no. 1: 71–82.

———. 2014. "Spirit Mediums in Hong Kong and the United States." In *Talking with the Spirits: Ethnographies from Between the Worlds,* edited by J. Hunter and D. Luke, 301–323. Brisbane, Australia: Daily Grail Publishing. http://www.dailygrail.com/Spirit-World/2014/3/Talking-the-Spirits-Ethnographies-Between-the-Worlds

Emmons, C. F., and P. Emmons. 2003. *Guided by Spirit: A Journey into the Mind of the Medium.* Lincoln, NE: iUniverse.

Evard, R. 2015. "The Paradigmatic Breakdown: A Model to Define the ExE Dynamics." *Journal of Exceptional Experiences and Psychology* 3, no. 1: 19–29.

Evard, R., and A. Ventola. 2018. *Mindfield. The Language of Our Field.* Durham, NC: Parapsychological Association.

Facco, E., E. Casiglia, B. Emanuel, A. Khafaji, F. Finatti, G. M. Duma, G. Mento, L. Pederzoli, and P. Tressoldi. 2019. "The Neurophenomenology of Out-of-Body Experiences Induced by Hypnotic Suggestions." *International Journal of Clinical and Experimental Hypnosis* 67, no. 1: 39–68.

Ferrer, J. N. 2000. "The Perennial Philosophy Revisited." *Journal of Transpersonal Psychology* 32, no. 1: 7–30.

Fontana, D. 2005. *Is There an Afterlife? A Comprehensive Overview of the Evidence.* Oakland, CA: O Books.

———. 2009. *Life Beyond Death: What Should We Expect?* London: Watkins Media Limited.

Fox, J. W. 1992. "The Structure, Stability, and Social Antecedents of Reported Paranormal Experiences." *Sociology of Religion* 53, no. 4: 417–431. https://doi.org/10.2307/3711436

French, C. C., and A. Stone. 2013. *Anomalistic Psychology: Exploring Paranormal Belief and Experience.* New York: Macmillan International Higher Education.

Galak, J., R. A. LeBoeuf, L. D. Nelson, and J. P. Simmons. 2012. "Correcting the Past: Failures to Replicate Psi." *Journal of Personality and Social Psychology* 103, no. 6: 933.

Gallup, G. H., and F. Newport. 1991. "Belief in Paranormal Phenomena Among Adult Americans." *Skeptical Inquirer* 15, no. 2: 137–146.

Gallup, Inc. 2005. "Three in Four Americans Believe in Paranormal: Little Change from Similar Results in 2001." (June 16). https://news.gallup.com/poll/16915/Three-Four-Americans-Believe-Paranormal.aspx

Gilbert, H. 2010. "A Sociological Perspective on 'Becoming' a Spirit Medium in Britain." *Rhine Online: Psi-News Magazine* 2 no. 1: 16–21.

———. 2014. "An Agnostic Social Scientific Perspective on Spirit Medium Experience in Great Britain." In *Talking with the Spirits: Ethnographies from Between the Worlds,* edited by J. Hunter and D. Luke, 57–71. Brisbane, Australia: Daily Grail Publishing.

Glicksohn, J. 1990. "Belief in the Paranormal and Subjective Paranormal Experience." *Personality and Individual Differences* 11, no. 7: 675–683.

Goff, P. 2019. *Galileo's Error: Foundations for a New Science of Consciousness.* New York: Pantheon.

Goulding, A. 2004. "Schizotypy Models in Relation to Subjective Health and Paranormal Beliefs and Experiences." *Personality and Individual Differences* 37, no. 1: 157–167.

————. 2005. "Healthy Schizotypy in a Population of Paranormal Believers and Experiments." *Personality and Individual Differences* 38, no. 5: 1069–1083.

Greeley, A. M. 1975. *The Sociology of the Paranormal: A Reconnaissance.* Thousand Oaks: Sage Publications, 23.

Greeley, A. 1987. "Mysticism Goes Mainstream." *American Health* 7: 47–49.

Griffiths, R. R., W. A. Richards, M. W. Johnson, U. D. McCann, and R. Jesse. 2008. "Mystical-Type Experiences Occasioned by Psilocybin Mediate the Attribution of Personal Meaning and Spiritual Significance 14 Months Later." *Journal of Psychopharmacology* 22, no. 6: 621–632. https://doi.org/10.1177/0269881108094300

Guggenheim, B., and J. Guggenheim. 2012. *Hello from Heaven: A New Field of Research—After-Death Communication Confirms That Life and Love Are Eternal.* New York: Bantam.

Guiley, R. E. 2010. *Spirit Communications.* New York: Chelsea House Publishers.

Hackett, C., B. J. Grim, and N. Kuriakose. 2012. "The Global Religious Landscape: A Report on the Size and Distribution of the World's Major Religious Groups as of 2010." Global Religious Futures Project. Washington, DC: Pew Research Center's Forum on Religion and Public Life.

Hageman, J. H., S. Krippner, and I. Wickramasekera. 2011. "Across Cultural Boundaries: Psychophysiological Responses, Absorption, and Dissociation Comparison Between Brazilian Spiritists and Advanced Meditators." *Neuroquantology* 9, no. 1.

Hageman, J. H., J. F. P. Peres, A. Moreira-Almeida, L. Caixeta, I. Wickramasekera, and S. C. Krippner. 2009. "The Neurobiology of Trance and Mediumship in Brazil." In *Mysterious Minds: The Neurobiology of Psychics, Mediums, and Other Extraordinary People,* edited by S. C. Krippner and H. L. Friedman. Westport, CT: Praeger.

Haraldsson, E. 1985. "Representative National Surveys of Psychic Phenomena: Iceland, Great Britain, Sweden, USA, and Gallup's Multinational Survey." *Journal of the Society for Psychical Research* 53, no. 801: 145–158.

————. 2005. "West- and East-Europeans and Their Belief in Reincarnation and Life After Death." *Romania* 28: 68.

————. 2011. "Psychic Experiences a Third of a Century Apart: Two Representative Surveys in Iceland with an International Comparison." *Journal of the Society for Psychical Research* 75, no. 903: 76.

Haraldsson, E., and J. M. Houtkooper. 1991. "Psychic Experiences in the Multinational Human Values Study: Who Reports Them." *Journal of the American Society for Psychical Research* 85, no. 2: 145–165.

Harary, K., and R. Targ. 1985. "A New Approach to Forecasting Commodity Futures." *Psi Research* 4, no. 3–4: 79–88.

Harrison, A., and J. Singer. 2013. "Boundaries in the Mind: Historical Context and Current Research Using the Boundary Questionnaire." *Imagination, Cognition, and Personality* 33, no. 1: 205–215.

Hastings, A. 1991. *With the Tongues of Men and Angels: A Study of Channeling.* New York: Harcourt School.

Helfrich, P. M. 2009. "The Channeling Phenomenon: A Multi-Methodological Assessment." *Journal of Integral Theory and Practice* 4, no. 3: 141–161.

Hitchman, G. A. M., C. A. Roe, and S. J. Sherwood. 2012. "A Reexamination of Nonintentional Precognition with Openness to Experience, Creativity, Psi Beliefs, and Luck Beliefs as Predictors of Success." *The Journal of Parapsychology* 76, no. 1: 109.

Hodgkinson, G. P., J. Langan-Fox, and E. Sadler-Smith. 2008. "Intuition: A Fundamental Bridging Construct in the Behavioural Sciences." *British Journal of Psychology* 99, no. 1: 1–27. https://doi.org/10.1348/000712607X216666

Höllinger, F., and T. B. Smith. 2002. "Religion and Esotericism Among Students: A Cross-Cultural Comparative Study." *Journal of Contemporary Religion* 17, no. 2: 229–249.

Holtgraves, T., and G. Stockdale. 1997. "The Assessment of Dissociative Experiences in a Non-Clinical Population: Reliability, Validity, and Factor Structure of the Dissociative Experiences Scale." *Personality and Individual Differences* 22, no. 5: 699–706.

Honorton, C., D. C. Ferrari, and D. J. Bem. 1998. "Extraversion and ESP Performance: A Meta-Analysis and a New Confirmation, 62, 255, 1998." *Journal of Parapsychology* 63, no. 1: 96–96.

Honorton, C., D. C. Ferrari, and G. Hansen. 2018. "Meta-Analysis of Forced-Choice Precognition Experiments (1935–1987)." *The Star Gate Archives: Reports of the United States Government Sponsored Psi Program, 1972–1995. Volume 2: Remote Viewing, 1985–1995,* 291.

Hubbard, G. S., and G. O. Langford. 1986. "A Suggested Remote Viewing Training Procedure." Central Intelligence Agency. https://www.cia.gov/library/readingroom/docs/CIA-RDP96-00787R000300110001-8.pdf

Hughes, D. J. 1991. "Blending with an Other: An Analysis of Trance Channeling in the United States." *Ethos* 19, no. 2: 161–184.

Hunter, J. 2014. "Mediumship and Folk Models of Mind and Matter." In *Talking with the Spirits: Ethnographies from Between the Worlds,* edited by J. Hunter and D. Luke, 99–129. Brisbane, Australia: Daily Grail Publishing.

Hunter, J., and D. Luke. 2014. *Talking with the Spirits: Ethnographies from Between the Worlds.* Brisbane, Australia: Daily Grail Publishing.

IBISWorld. 2019. "Industry Market Research, Reports, and Statistics." (December 31). https://www.ibisworld.com/default.aspx

Irwin, H. J. 1993. "Belief in the Paranormal: A Review of the Empirical Literature." *Journal of the American Society for Psychical Research* 87, no. 1: 1–39.

————. 2009. *The Psychology of Paranormal Belief: A Researcher's Handbook*. Hatfield, England: University of Hertfordshire Press.

Irwin, H. J. 2017. "Empathy and Parapsychological Experiences: A Constructive Replication." *Journal of the Society for Psychical Research* 81, no. 1.

Jahn, R. G., B. J. Dunne, R. G. Nelson, Y. H. Dobyns, and G. J. Bradish. 2007. "Correlations of Random Binary Sequences with Pre-Stated Operator Intention: A Review of a 12-Year Program." *Explore* 3, no. 3: 244–253.

Jain, S., R. Hammerschlag, P. Mills, L. Cohen, R. Krieger, C. Vieten, and S. Lutgendorf. 2015. "Clinical Studies of Biofield Therapies: Summary, Methodological Challenges, and Recommendations." *Global Advances in Health and Medicine* 4 (Supplement): 58–66. https://doi.org/10.7453/gahmj.2015.034.suppl

Kawai, N., M. Honda, S. Nakamura, P. Samatra, K. Sukardika, Y. Nakatani, N. Shimojo, and T. Oohashi. 2001. "Catecholamines and Opioid Peptides Increase in Plasma in Humans During Possession Trances." *Neuroreport* 12, no. 16: 3419–3423.

Kawai, N., M. Honda, E. Nishina, R. Yagi, and T. Oohashi. 2017. "Electroencephalogram Characteristics During Possession Trances in Healthy Individuals." *Neuroreport* 28, no. 15: 949.

Kean, L. 2018. *Surviving Death: A Journalist Investigates Evidence for an Afterlife*. New York: Three Rivers Press.

Kelly, F. C. 2014. "A Study in Human Incredulity." http://www.wright-brothers.org /History_Wing/Aviations_Attic/They_Wouldnt_Believe/They_Wouldnt_Believe _the_Wrights_Had_Flown.htm

Kennedy, J. E. 1995. "Methods for Investigating Goal-Oriented Psi." *Journal of Parapsychology* 59: 47–62.

Kennedy, J. E., and H. Kanthamani. 1995a. "An Exploratory Study of the Effects of Paranormal and Spiritual Experiences on Peoples' Lives and Well-Being." *Journal of the American Society for Psychical Research* 89, no. 3: 249–264.

————. 1995b. "Association between Anomalous Experiences and Artistic Creativity and Spirituality." *Journal of the American Society for Psychical Research* 89: 333–43.

Kharusi, L. 2019. Personal communication.

————. 2020. "Dira International." Dira. https://www.dirainternational.com/

Kihlstrom, J. F. 2005. "Dissociative Disorders." *Annual Review of Clinical Psychology* 1: 227–253.

Kiznys, D., J. Vencloviene, and I. Milvidaité. 2020. "The Associations of Geomagnetic Storms, Fast Solar Wind, and Stream Interaction Regions with Cardiovascular Characteristic in Patients with Acute Coronary Syndrome." *Life Sciences in Space Research* 25: 1–8.

Klimo, J. 1998. *Channeling: Investigations on Receiving Information from Paranormal Sources*. Berkeley, CA: North Atlantic Books.

Kolodziejzyk, G. 2013. "Greg Kolodziejzyk's 13-Year Associative Remote Viewing Experiment Results." *Journal of Parapsychology* 76: 349–368.

Krippner, S. 2005. "Psychoneurological Dimensions of Anomalous Experience in Relation to Religious Belief and Spiritual Practice." In *Soul, Psyche, Brain: New Directions in the Study of Religion and Brain-Mind Science,* edited by K. Bulkeley, 61–92. New York: Springer.

———. 2008. "Learning from the Spirits: Candomblé, Umbanda, and Kardecismo in Recife, Brazil." *Anthropology of Consciousness* 19, no. 1: 1–32.

Lange, R., M. A. Thalbourne, J. Houran, and L. Storm. 2000. "The Revised Transliminality Scale: Reliability and Validity Data from a Rasch Top-Down Purification Procedure." *Conscious Cognition* 9, no. 4: 591–617. https://doi.org /10.1006/ccog.2000.0472

Lawrence, T. 1993. "Bringing Home the Sheep: A Meta-Analysis of Sheep/Goat Experiments." In Proceedings of the 36th Annual Parapsychology Convention.

Leavitt, F. 1999. "Dissociative Experiences Scale Taxon and Measurement of Dissociative Pathology: Does the Taxon Add to an Understanding of Dissociation and Its Associated Pathologies?" *Journal of Clinical Psychology in Medical Settings* 6, no. 4: 427–240.

Lerchl, A., K. O. Nonaka, and R. J. Reiter. 1991. "Pineal Gland 'Magnetosensitivity' to Static Magnetic Fields Is a Consequence of Induced Electric Currents (Eddy Currents)." *Journal of Pineal Research* 10, no. 3: 109–116. https://doi.org/10.1111 /j.1600-079x.1991.tb00826.x

Levin, J. 2016. "Prevalence and Religious Predictors of Healing Prayer Use in the USA: Findings from the Baylor Religion Survey." *Journal of Religion and Health* 55, no. 4: 1136–1158.

Lewis-Fernandez, R. 1998. "A Cultural Critique of the *DSM-IV* Dissociative Disorders Section." *Transcultural Psychiatry* 35, no. 3: 387–400.

Lindeman, M., and K. Aarnio. 2006. "Paranormal Beliefs: Their Dimensionality and Correlates." *European Journal of Personality* 20, no. 7: 585–602.

Lipka, M., and C. Gecewicz. 2017. "More Americans Now Say They're Spiritual but Not Religious." *Pew Research Center* (blog). Accessed May 3, 2020. https://www .pewresearch.org/fact-tank/2017/09/06/more-americans-now-say-theyre-spiritual -but-not-religious/

Lokhorst, G.-J. 2018. "Descartes and the Pineal Gland." In *The Stanford Encyclopedia of Philosophy,* edited by E. N. Zalta. (Winter). Stanford, CA: Metaphysics Research Lab, Stanford University. https://plato.stanford.edu/archives/win2018/entries /pineal-gland/

Lomas, T., I. Ivtzan, and C. H. Fu. 2015. "A Systematic Review of the Neurophysiology of Mindfulness on EEG Oscillations." *Neuroscience & Biobehavioral Reviews* 57 (October): 401–410. https://doi.org/10.1016/j.neubiorev.2015.09.018

Luke, D. 2012. "Psychoactive Substances and Paranormal Phenomena: A Comprehensive Review." *International Journal of Transpersonal Studies* 31: 97–156.

————. 2014. "Psychedelic Possession: The Growing Incorporation of Incorporation into Ayahuasca Use." In *Talking with the Spirits: Ethnographies from between the Worlds*, edited by J. Hunter and D. Luke, 229–254. Brisbane, Australia: Daily Grail Publishing. http://www.dailygrail.com/Spirit-World/2014/3/Talking-the-Spirits -Ethnographies-Between-the-Worlds

————. 2015. "Drugs and Psi Phenomena." In *Parapsychology: A Handbook for the 21st Century*, edited by E. Cardeña, J. Palmer, and D. Marcusson-Clavertz, 149–164. Jefferson, NC: McFarland & Company.

Luke, D. P., C. A. Roe, and J. Davison. 2008. "Testing for Forced-Choice Precognition Using a Hidden Task: Two Replications." *The Journal of Parapsychology* 72: 133.

Lukoff, D. 2010. "Visionary Spiritual Experiences." In *Psychosis and Spirituality*, edited by I. Clarke, 205–215. New York: John Wiley & Sons. https://doi.org/10 .1002/9780470970300.ch16

MacDonald, W. L. 1995. "The Effects of Religiosity and Structural Strain on Reported Paranormal Experiences." *Journal for the Scientific Study of Religion* 34, no. 3: 366–376. https://doi.org/10.2307/1386885

Machado, F. R. 2010. "Experiências anômalas (motor extra-sensorial) na vida diária e sua associação com crenças, atitudes e bem-estar subjetivo [Anomalous Experiences (extrasensorymotor) in daily life and their association with beliefs, attitudes and subjective well-being]." *Boletim Academia Paulista de Psicologia* 30, no. 79: 462–483.

Mander, W. 2020. "Pantheism." In *The Stanford Encyclopedia of Philosophy*, edited by E. N. Zalta. (Spring). Stanford, CA: Metaphysics Research Lab, Stanford University. https://plato.stanford.edu/archives/spr2020/entries/pantheism/

Maraldi, E., and M. F. Fernandes. 2020. "Luiz Antônio Gasparetto." Psi Encyclopedia. London: The Society for Psychical Research. https://psi-encyclopedia.spr.ac.uk /articles/luiz-ant%C3%B4nio-gasparetto

Maraldi, E., W. Zangari, F. R. Machado, and S. Krippner. 2014. "Anomalous Mental and Physical Phenomena of Brazilian Mediums: A Review of the Scientific Literature." In *Talking with the Spirits: Ethnographies from Between the Worlds*, edited by J. Hunter and D. Luke, 175–212. Brisbane, Australia: Daily Grail Publishing.

May, E. C., and S. B. Marwaha. 2018a. *The Star Gate Archives: Reports of the United States Government Sponsored Psi Program, 1972–1995.* Volume 1. Jefferson, NC: McFarland & Company.

————. 2018b. *The Star Gate Archives: Reports of the United States Government Sponsored Psi Program, 1972–1995. Volume 2: Remote Viewing, 1985–1995.* Volume. 2. Jefferson, NC: McFarland & Company.

May, E. C., J. Utts, and S. J. P. Spottiswoode. 1995. "Decision Augmentation Theory: Toward a Model of Anomalous Mental Phenomena." *Journal of Parapsychology* 59: 195–220.

McClenon, J. 1993. "Surveys of Anomalous Experience in Chinese, Japanese, and American Samples." *Sociology of Religion* 54, no. 3: 295–302.

McKie, D., and G. R. De Beer. n.d. "Netwon's Apple." *Notes and Records Royal Society Journal of the History of Science* 9. https://doi.org/10.1098/rsnr.1951.0003

McNamara, S. 2019a. "Mind Possible: With Sean McNamara." Mind Possible with Sean McNamara. https://www.mindpossible.com/

———. 2019b. Personal communication.

Millar, B. 2015. "Quantum Theory and Parapsychology." In *Parapsychology: A Handbook for the 21st Century,* edited by E. Cardeña, J. Palmer, and D. Marcusson-Clavertz, 165–180. Jefferson, NC: McFarland & Company.

Miller, R-E L., and H. Wahbeh. 2018. "Terms and Definitions for Subjective Information Reception from Discarnate Beings: A Systematic Review." Non-peer reviewed manuscript. Research Gate. https://www.researchgate.net/publication/338925036 _Terms_and_definitions_for_subjective_information_reception_from_discarnate _beings_A_systematic_review_Authors

Milton, J. 1997. "Meta-Analysis of Free-Response ESP Studies Without Altered States of Consciousness." *Journal of Parapsychology* 61: 279–319.

Moore, D. W. 2005. "Three in Four Americans Believe in Paranormal." (June 16). http://www.gallup.com/poll/16915/three-four-americans-believe-paranormal.aspx

Moore, R. 1970. "Spiritualism and Society." *Sociology* 4, no. 1: 138–139.

Moreira-Almeida, A., and E. Cardeña. 2011. "Differential Diagnosis Between Non-Pathological Psychotic and Spiritual Experiences and Mental Disorders: A Contribution from Latin American Studies to the ICD-11." *Brazilian Journal of Psychiatry* 33 (Supplement 1).

Moreira-Almeida, A., A. A. S. de Almeida, and F. L. Neto. 2005. "History of 'Spiritist Madness' in Brazil." *History of Psychiatry* 16, no. 1: 5–25. https://doi. org/10.1177/0957154X05044602

Moreira-Almeida, A., and J. D. Koss-Chioino. 2009. "Recognition and Treatment of Psychotic Symptoms: Spiritists Compared to Mental Health Professionals in Puerto Rico and Brazil." *Psychiatry: Interpersonal and Biological Processes* 72, no. 3: 268–283. https://doi.org/10.1521/psyc.2009.72.3.268

Moreira-Almeida, A., F. L. Neto, and E. Cardeña. 2008. "Comparison of Brazilian Spiritist Mediumship and Dissociative Identity Disorder." *The Journal of Nervous and Mental Disease* 196, no. 5: 420–424.

Moreira-Almeida, A., F. L. Neto, and B. Greyson. 2007. "Dissociative and Psychotic Experiences in Brazilian Spiritist Mediums." *Psychotherapy and Psychosomatics* 76, no. 1: 57–58. https://doi.org/10.1159/000096365

Mossbridge, J., and D. Radin. 2017. "Precognition as a Form of Prospection: A Review of the Evidence." *Psychology of Consciousness: Theory, Research, and Practice.* In press.

Mossbridge, J., P. Tressoldi, and J. Utts. 2012. "Predictive Physiological Anticipation Preceding Seemingly Unpredictable Stimuli: A Meta-Analysis." *Frontiers in Psychology* 3.

Mossbridge, J., P. Tressoldi, J. Utts, J. A. Ives, D. Radin, and W. B. Jonas. 2014. "Predicting the Unpredictable: Critical Analysis and Practical Implications of Predictive Anticipatory Activity." *Frontiers in Human Neuroscience* 8: 146.

Mulder, R. T., A. L. Beautrais, P. R. Joyce, and D. M. Fergusson. 1998. "Relationship Between Dissociation, Childhood Sexual Abuse, Childhood Physical Abuse, and Mental Illness in a General Population Sample." *American Journal of Psychiatry* 155, no. 6: 806–811.

National Alliance on Mental Illness. 2017. "Dissociative Disorders." https://www .nami.org/Learn-More/Mental-Health-Conditions/Dissociative-Disorders

Negro, P. J., Jr., P. Palladino-Negro, and M. R. Louzã. 2002. "Do Religious Mediumship Dissociative Experiences Conform to the Sociocognitive Theory of Dissociation?" *Journal of Trauma & Dissociation* 3, no. 1: 51–73.

Nelson, R. D. 1997. "Multiple Field REG/RNG Recordings During a Global Event." *Electronic Journal for Anomalous Phenomena.*

———. 2015. "Implicit Physical Psi: The Global Consciousness Project." In *Parapsychology: A Handbook for the 21st Century*, edited by E. Cardeña, J. Palmer, and D. Marcusson-Clavertz, 1: 282–292. Jefferson, NC: McFarland & Company.

Nelson, R. D., G. J. Bradish, Y. H. Dobyns, B. J. Dunne, and R. G. Jahn. 1996. "FieldREG Anomalies in Group Situations." *Journal of Scientific Exploration* 10, no. 1: 111–141.

Nishimura, T., I-J Tsai, H. Yamauchi, E. Nakatani, M. Fukushima, and C. Y. Hsu. 2020. "Association of Geomagnetic Disturbances and Suicide Attempts in Taiwan, 1997–2013: A Cross-Sectional Study." *International Journal of Environmental Research and Public Health* 17, no. 4: 1154.

Nuevo, R., S. Chatterji, E. Verdes, N. Naidoo, C. Arango, and J. L. Ayuso-Mateos. 2012. "The Continuum of Psychotic Symptoms in the General Population: A Cross-National Study." *Schizophrenia Bulletin* 38, no. 3: 475–485. https://doi .org/10.1093/schbul/sbq099

O'Regan, B. and C. Hirshberg. 1993. *Spontaneous Remission: An Annotated Bibliography.* Sausalito, CA: Institute of Noetic Sciences.

Ogawa, J. R., L. A. Sroufe, N. S. Weinfield, E. A. Carlson, and B. Egeland. 1997. "Development and the Fragmented Self: Longitudinal Study of Dissociative Symptomatology in a Nonclinical Sample." *Development and Psychopathology* 9449009 9, no. 4: 855–879.

Oman, D. 2018. "Religious/Spiritual Effects on Physical Morbidity and Mortality." In *Why Religion and Spirituality Matter for Public Health: Evidence, Implications, and Resources*, edited by D. Oman, 65–79. New York: Springer International Publishing. https://doi.org/10.1007/978-3-319-73966-3_4

Oohashi, T., N. Kawai, M. Honda, S. Nakamura, M. Morimoto, E. Nishina, and T. Maekawa. 2002. "Electroencephalographic Measurement of Possession Trance in the Field." *Clinical Neurophysiology* 113, no. 3: 435–445.

Orenstein, A. 2002. "Religion and Paranormal Belief." *Journal for the Scientific Study of Religion* 41, no. 2: 301–311.

Otis, L. P., and J. E. Alcock. 1982. "Factors Affecting Extraordinary Belief." *The Journal of Social Psychology* 118, no. 1: 77–85.

Palmer, G., and W. Braud. 2002. "Exceptional Human Experiences, Disclosure, and a More Inclusive View of Physical, Psychological, and Spiritual Well-Being." *Journal of Transpersonal Psychology* 34, no. 1: 29–59.

Palmer, J. 1979. "A Community Mail Survey of Psychic Experiences." *Journal of the American Society for Psychical Research* 73, no. 3: 221–251.

Pederzoli, L., E. Prati, N. Resti, D. Del Carlo, and P. E. Tressoldi. 2018. "Hypno-Channelings: A New Tool for the Investigation of Channeling Experiences." *Available at SSRN 3281560.*

Peres, J. F., A. Moreira-Almeida, L. Caixeta, F. Leao, and A. Newberg. 2012. "Neuroimaging During Trance State: A Contribution to the Study of Dissociation." *PLoS One* 7, no. 11: e49360. https://doi.org/10.1371/journal.pone.0049360

Pew Research Center. 2009. "Supernatural Experiences." http://pewrsr.ch/1PUw3wX

Plakun, E. M. 2008. "Psychiatry in Tibetan Buddhism: Madness and Its Cure Seen Through the Lens of Religious and National History." *The Journal of the American Academy of Psychoanalysis and Dynamic Psychiatry* 36, no. 3: 415–430. https://doi.org/10.1521/jaap.2008.36.3.415

Rabeyron, T., and T. Loose. 2015. "Anomalous Experiences, Trauma, and Symbolization Processes at the Frontiers between Psychoanalysis and Cognitive Neurosciences." *Frontiers in Psychology* 6: 1926.

Rabeyron, T., and C. A. Watt. 2010. "Paranormal Experiences, Mental Health and Mental Boundaries, and Psi." *Personality and Individual Differences* 48, no. 4: 487–492. https://doi.org/10.1016/j.paid.2009.11.029

Radin, D. 2006. "Experiments Testing Models of Mind-Matter Interaction." *Journal of Scientific Exploration* 20, no. 3: 27.

———. 2013. *Supernormal: Science, Yoga, and the Evidence for Extraordinary Psychic Abilities.* New York: Random House.

———. 2018. "Collective Consciousness at Burning Man." Institute of Noetic Sciences Digital Media Library. https://library.noetic.org/library/video-interviews/collective-consciousness-burning-man-overview-research

Radin, D., and D. Ferrari. 1991. "Effects of Consciousness on the Fall of Dice: A Meta-Analysis." *Journal of Scientific Exploration* 5, no. 1: 61–83.

Radin, D., R. Nelson, Y. H. Dobyns, and J. Houtkooper. 2006. "Assessing the Evidence for Mind-Matter Interaction Effects." *Journal of Scientific Exploration* 30, no. 3: 361–374.

Radin, D., and A. Pierce. 2015. "Psi and Psychophysiology." In *Parapsychology: A Handbook for the 21st Century,* edited by E. Cardeña, J. Palmer, and D. Marcusson-Clavertz. Jefferson, NC: McFarland & Company. https://psycnet .apa.org/record/2015-48721-017

Rakovic, D. 2010. "On Nature and Control of Creativity—Tesla as a Case Study." In *Second International Workshop on Knowledge Federation,* 6. Dubrovnik, Croatia.

Randrup, A. 2003. "The Perennial Philosophy." *The International Journal of Transpersonal Studies* 22: 120–121.

Rao, A., L. D. Hickman, D. Sibbritt, P. J. Newton, and J. L. Phillips. 2016. "Is Energy Healing an Effective Non-Pharmacological Therapy for Improving Symptom Management of Chronic Illnesses? A Systematic Review." *Complementary Therapies in Clinical Practice* 25: 26–41.

Rapoport, R., D. Leiby-Clark, and E. Czyzewicz. 2017. "Methodology Report: American Fears Survey July 2017." Glen Mills, PA: Chapman University. https:// www.chapman.edu/wilkinson/research-centers/babbie-center/_files/Chapman -Survey-of-America-Fears-methodology.pdf

———. 2018. "Methodology Report: American Fears Survey July 2018." Glen Mills, PA: Chapman University.

Rattet, S. L., and K. Bursik. 2001. "Investigating the Personality Correlates of Paranormal Belief and Precognitive Experience." *Personality and Individual Differences* 31, no. 3: 433–444.

Rauch, D., J. Handsteiner, A. Hochrainer, J. Gallicchio, A. S. Friedman, C. Leung, B. Liu, et al. 2018. "Cosmic Bell Test Using Random Measurement Settings from High-Redshift Quasars." *Physical Review Letters* 121, no. 8: 080403. https://doi .org/10.1103/PhysRevLett.121.080403

Reed, H. 1989. *Edgar Cayce on Channeling Your Higher Self.* New York: ARE Press.

Reed, H., and C. T. Cayce. 2007. *Edgar Cayce on Channeling Your Higher Self.* New York: ARE Press.

Richards, D. G. 1991. "A Study of the Correlations Between Subjective Psychic Experiences and Dissociative Experiences." *Dissociation: Progress in the Dissociative Disorders* 4, no. 2: 83–91.

Richards, T. L., L. Kozak, L. C. Johnson, and L. J. Standish. 2005. "Replicable Functional Magnetic Resonance Imaging. Evidence of Correlated Brain Signals Between Physically and Sensory-Isolated Subjects." *Journal of Alternative and Complementary Medicine* 11, no. 6: 955–963.

Ritchie, S. J., R. Wiseman, and C. C. French. 2012. "Failing the Future: Three Unsuccessful Attempts to Replicate Bem's 'Retroactive Facilitation of Recall' Effect." *PloS One* 7, no. 3.

Rocha, A. C., D. Paraná, E. S. Freire, F. L. Neto, and A. Moreira-Almeida. 2014. "Investigating the Fit and Accuracy of Alleged Mediumistic Writing: A Case Study of Chico Xavier's Letters." *Explore* 10, no. 5: 300–308. https://doi.org /10.1016/j.explore.2014.06.002

Rock, A. J., J. Beischel, and C. C. Cott. 2009. "Psi vs. Survival: A Qualitative Investigation of Mediums' Phenomenology Comparing Psychic Readings and Ostensible Communication with the Deceased." *Transpersonal Psychology Review* 13, no. 2: 76–89.

Rock, A. J., E. B. Thorsteinsson, P. E. Tressoldi, and N. M. Loi. 2020. "A Meta-Analysis of Anomalous Information Reception by Mediums: Assessing the Forced-Choice Design in Mediumship Research, 2000–2019." *Advances in Parapsychological Research* 10.

Roe, C. A. 1998. "Belief in the Paranormal and Attendance at Psychic Readings." *Journal of the American Society for Psychical Research* 92, no. 1: 25–51.

Roe, C. A., S. J. Henderson, and J. Matthews. 2008. "Extraversion and Performance at a Forced-Choice ESP Task with Verbal Stimuli: Two Studies." *Journal of the Society for Psychical Research* 72, no. 893: 208–220.

Roe, C. A., C. Sonnex, and E. C. Roxburgh. 2015. "Two Meta-Analyses of Noncontact Healing Studies." *Explore* 11, no. 1: 11–23.

Roman, S., and D. Packer. 1989. *Opening to Channel: How to Connect with Your Guide.* HJ Kramer.

Roney-Dougal, S. M. 1989. "Recent Findings Relating to the Possible Role of the Pineal Gland in Affecting Psychic Ability." *Journal of the Society for Psychical Research* 55, no. 815: 313–328.

———. 2015. "Ariadne's Thread: Meditation and Psi." *Parapsychology: A Handbook for the 21st Century*, edited by E. Cardeña, J. Palmer, and D. Marcusson-Clavertz, 125. Jefferson, NC: McFarland & Company.

Roney-Dougal, S. M., and G. Vogl. 1993. "Some Speculations on the Effect of Geomagnetism on the Pineal Gland." *Journal of the Society for Psychical Research* 59: no. 1–1.

Ross, C. A., and S. Joshi. 1992. "Paranormal Experiences in the General Population." *The Journal of Nervous and Mental Disease* 180, no. 6: 357–361.

Roxburgh, E. C., and C. A. Roe. 2011. "A Survey of Dissociation, Boundary Thinness, and Psychological Wellbeing in Spiritualist Mental Mediumship." *The Journal of Parapsychology* 75, no. 2: 279.

Ryan, A. 2015. "Physical Correlates of Psi." *Parapsychology: A Handbook for the 21st Century*, edited by E. Cardeña, J. Palmer, and D. Marcusson-Clavertz, 181–191. Jefferson, NC: McFarland & Company.

Sagher, A., B. Butzer, and H. Wahbeh. 2019. "The Characteristics of Exceptional Human Experiences." *Journal of Consciousness Studies* 26, no. 11–12: 203–237.

Sarraf, M. A., M. A. Woodley, and P. Tressoldi. 2020. "Anomalous Information Reception by Mediums: A Meta-Analysis of the Scientific Evidence." *Explore.* In press.

Schmidt, H. 1974. "Comparison of PK Action on Two Different Random Number Generators." *The Journal of Parapsychology* 38, no. 1: 47.

———. 1987. "The Strange Properties of Psychokinesis." *Journal of Scientific Exploration* 1, no. 2: 103–118.

Schmidt, S. 2012. "Can We Help Just by Good Intentions? A Meta-Analysis of Experiments on Distant Intention Effects." *The Journal of Alternative and Complementary Medicine* 18, no. 6: 529–533.

———. 2015. "Experimental Research on Distant Intention Phenomena." *Parapsychology: A Handbook for the 21st Century*, edited by E. Cardeña, J. Palmer, and D. Marcusson-Clavertz, 244–257. Jefferson, NC: McFarland & Company.

Schmidt, S., R. Schneider, J. Utts, and H. Walach. 2004. "Distant Intentionality and the Feeling of Being Stared At: Two Meta-Analyses." *British Journal of Psychology* 95, no. 2: 235–247.

Schofield, K., and G. Claridge. 2007. "Paranormal Experiences and Mental Health: Schizotypy as an Underlying Factor." *Personality and Individual Differences* 43, no. 7: 1908–1916.

Schooler, J. W., S. L. Baumgart, and M. Franklin. 2018. "Entertaining Without Endorsing: The Case for Scientific Investigation of Anomalous Cognition." *Psychology of Consciousness: Theory, Research, and Practice* 5, no. 1: 63–77.

Schouten, S. 1993. "Are We Making Progress." In *Psi Research Methodology: A Re-Examination, Proceedings of an International Conference, Oct 29-20, 1988*, edited by L. Coly and J. McMahon, NY: Parapsychology Foundation, Inc.

Schwartz, S. A. 1995. "Creativity, Intuition, and Innovation." *Subtle Energies & Energy Medicine Journal Archives* 1, no. 2.

———. 2005. *The Secret Vaults of Time: Psychic Archaeology and the Quest for Man's Beginnings*. Volume 12. Newburyport, MA: Hampton Roads Publishing.

———. 2017. *Remote Viewing the Future with Stephan A. Schwartz.* https://www.youtube.com/watch?v=avbsEEz98Ck

———. 2019. "The Location and Reconstruction of a Byzantine Structure in Marea, Egypt, Including a Comparison of Electronic Remote Sensing and Remote Viewing." *Journal of Scientific Exploration* 33, no. 3: 451–480.

Schwartz, S. A., R. J. De Mattei, and R, C. Smith. 2019. "The Caravel Project." *Zeitschrift Für Anomalistik Volume* 19: 113–139.

Seligman, R. 2005a. "Distress, Dissociation, and Embodied Experience: Reconsidering the Pathways to Mediumship and Mental Health." *Ethos* 33, no. 1: 71–99.

———. 2005b. "From Affliction to Affirmation: Narrative Transformation and the Therapeutics of Candomblé Mediumship." *Transcultural Psychiatry* 42, no. 2: 272–294.

Seligman, R., and L. J. Kirmayer. 2008. "Dissociative Experience and Cultural Neuroscience: Narrative, Metaphor and Mechanism." *Culture, Medicine and Psychiatry* 32, no. 1: 31–64.

Sheils, D., and P. Berg. 1977. "A Research Note on Sociological Variables Related to Belief in Psychic Phenomena." *Wisconsin Sociologist* 14, no. 1: 24–31.

Sheldrake, R. 2015. "Psi in Everyday Life." *Parapsychology: A Handbook for the 21st Century*, edited by E. Cardeña, J. Palmer, and D. Marcusson-Clavertz, 350. Jefferson, NC: McFarland & Company.

Sidky, H. 2018. "The War on Science, Anti-Intellectualism, and Alternative Ways of Knowing in 21st-Century America." *Skeptical Inquirer* 42, no. 2: 38–43.

Sigelman, L. 1977. "Multi-Nation Surveys of Religious Beliefs." *Journal for the Scientific Study of Religion*, 289–294.

Sinclair, M., and N. M. Ashkanasy. 2005. "Intuition: Myth or a Decision-Making Tool?" *Management Learning* 36, no. 3: 353–370. https://doi.org/10.1177/1350507605055351

Sjödin, U. 1995. "Paranormal Beliefs Among Swedish Youth." *Young* 3, no. 2: 46–57.

Smith, C. C., D. Laham, and J. Moddel. 2014. "Stock Market Prediction Using Associative Remote Viewing by Inexperienced Remote Viewers." *Journal of Scientific Exploration* 28: 7–16.

Snowman, C., and A. Scheuerle. 2009. "Qualitative Descriptors of Disease Incidence: Commonly Used and Frequently Muddled." *American Journal of Medical Genetics Part A* 149, no. 7: 1460–1462.

Sørensen, K. 2016. "The Psychosynthesis Model of the Personality." In *The Soul of Psychosynthesis: The Seven Core Concepts,* 192. Kentaur Publishing. https://kennethsorensen.dk/en/the-psychosynthesis-model-of-the-personality/

Spinelli, S. N., H. M. Reid, and J. M. Norvilitis. 2002. "Belief in and Experience with the Paranormal: Relations Between Personality Boundaries, Executive Functioning, Gender Role, and Academic Variables." *Imagination, Cognition, and Personality* 21, no. 4: 333–346.

Spitzer, C., S. Barnow, H. J. Freyberger, and H. J. Grabe. 2006. "Recent Developments in the Theory of Dissociation." *World Psychiatry* 5, no. 2: 82–86.

Stanford, R. G. 2015. "Psychological Concepts of Psi Function." *Parapsychology: A Handbook for the 21st Century*, edited by E. Cardeña, J. Palmer, and D. Marcusson-Clavertz, 94–109. Jefferson, NC: McFarland & Company.

Stolovy, T., R. Lev-Wiesel, and E. Witztum. 2015. "Dissociation: Adjustment or Distress? Dissociative Phenomena, Absorption, and Quality of Life Among Israeli Women Who Practice Channeling Compared to Women with Similar Traumatic History." *Journal of Religion and Health* 54, no. 3: 1040–1051.

198 The Science of Channeling

Storm, L., and P. Tressoldi. 2017. "Gathering in More Sheep and Goats: A Meta-Analysis of Forced-Choice Sheep-Goat ESP Studies, 1994–2015." *The Journal of the Society for Psychical Research* 81, no. 2: 79.

Storm, L., P. E. Tressoldi, and L. Di Risio. 2010. "Meta-Analysis of Free-Response Studies, 1992–2008: Assessing the Noise Reduction Model in Parapsychology." *Psychological Bulletin* 136, no. 4: 471–485. https://doi.org/10.1037/a0019457

Storm, L., and A. J. Rock. 2015. "Dreaming of Psi: A Narrative Review and Meta-Analysis of Dream-ESP Studies at the Maimonides Dream Laboratory and Beyond." In *Stanley Krippner: A Life of Dreams, Myths, and Visions. Essays on His Contributions and Influence*, edited by J. Davies and D. Pitchford. Colorado Springs: University Professors Press.

Storm, L., S. J. Sherwood, C. A. Roe, P. E. Tressoldi, A. J. Rock, and L. Di Risio. 2017. "On the Correspondence Between Dream Content and Target Material Under Laboratory Conditions: A Meta-Analysis of Dream-ESP Studies, 1966–2016." *International Journal of Dream Research*.

Storm, L., and P. E. Tressoldi. 2020. "Meta-Analysis of Free-Response Studies 2009–2018: Assessing the Noise-Reduction Model Ten Years On."

Storm, L., P. E. Tressoldi, and L. Di Risio. 2012. "Meta-Analysis of ESP Studies, 1987–2010: Assessing the Success of the Forced-Choice Design in Parapsychology." *Journal of Parapsychology* 76, no. 2: 243–273.

Swann, I. 2018. *Everybody's Guide to Natural ESP*. Swann-Ryder Productions, LLC.

Targ, R. 2019. "What Do We Know About Psi? The First Decade of Remote-Viewing Research and Operations at Stanford Research Institute." *Journal of Scientific Exploration* 33, no. 4: 569–592.

Tellegen, A., and G. Atkinson. 1974. "Openness to Absorbing and Self-Altering Experiences ('Absorption'), a Trait Related to Hypnotic Susceptibility." *Journal of Abnormal Psychology* 83, no. 3: 268–277.

Thalbourne, M. A. 2000. "Relation Between Transliminality and Openness to Experience." *Psychological Reports* 86, no. 3: 909–910.

———. 2003. *A Glossary of Terms Used in Parapsychology*. Puente Publications.

Traxler, M. J., D. J. Foss, R. Podali, and M. Zirnstein. 2012. "Feeling the Past: The Absence of Experimental Evidence for Anomalous Retroactive Influences on Text Processing." *Memory & Cognition* 40, no. 8: 1366–1372. https://doi.org/10.3758/s13421-012-0232-2

Tremmel, M. 2014. "Clarification of Terms and Concepts Defining Parapsychology and Related Disciplines: Comments on Mathijsen (2009, 2013), Abrassart (2013), and Evrard (2013)." *Journal of Exceptional Experiences and Psychology* 2, no. 1: 21–40.

———. 2015. "Clarification of Terms and Concepts Defining Parapsychology and Related Disciplines: Reply to Evrard (2014) and Update." *Journal of Exceptional Experiences and Psychology* 3, no. 1: 30–40.

van Lommel, P., R. van Wees, V. Meyers, and I. Elfferich. 2001. "Near-Death Experience in Survivors of Cardiac Arrest: A Prospective Study in the Netherlands." *Lancet* 358, no. 9298: 2039–2045. https://doi.org/10.1016/S0140-6736(01)07100-8

Varvoglis, M., and P. A. Bancel. 2015. "Micro-Psychokinesis." In *Parapsychology: A Handbook for the 21st Century*, edited by E. Cardeña, J. Palmer, and D. Marcusson-Clavertz, 266–281. Jefferson, NC: McFarland & Company.

Vieten, C., H. Wahbeh, B. Rael Cahn, K. MacLean, M. Estrada, P. Mills, M. Murphy, et al. 2018. "Future Directions in Meditation Research: Recommendations for Expanding the Field of Contemplative Science." *PLoS One* 13, no. 11: e0205740. https://doi.org/10.1371/journal.pone.0205740

Vigh, B., M. J. Manzano, A. Zádori, C. L. Frank, A. Lukáts, P. Röhlich, A. Szél, and C. Dávid. 2002. "Nonvisual Photoreceptors of the Deep Brain, Pineal Organs and Retina." *Histology and Histopathology* 17, no. 2: 555–590. https://doi.org/10.14670/HH-17.555

Vivekananda, S. 1893. *Vedanta Philosophy: Raja Yoga, Being Lectures by the Swami Vivekananda; with Patanjali's Aphorisms, Commentaries, and a Glossary of Terms (Google eBook)*. London: Kegan Paul, Trench, Trubner & Co., Ltd.

Wahbeh, H. 2020. "Spontaneous Remission Bibliography Project." Institute of Noetic Sciences (blog). 2020. https://noetic.org/research/spontaneous-remission-bibliography-project/

Wahbeh, H., and B. Butzer. 2020. "Characteristics of English-Speaking Trance Channelers." *Explore* 16, no. 5, 305–309. https://doi.org/10.1016/j.explore.2020.02.002

Wahbeh, H., C. Cannard, J. Okonsky, and A. Delorme. 2019. "A Physiological Examination of Perceived Incorporation During Trance." *F1000Research* 8 (January): 67. https://doi.org/10.12688/f1000research.17157.1

Wahbeh, H., L. Carpenter, and D. Radin. 2018. "A Mixed-Methods Phenomenological and Exploratory Study of Channeling." *Journal of the Society for Psychical Research* 82, no. 3: 129–148.

Wahbeh, H., K. McDermott, and A. Sagher. 2018. "Dissociative Symptoms and Anomalous Information Reception." *Activitas Nervosa Superior*, 1–11. https://doi.org/10.1007/s41470-018-0023-6

Wahbeh, H., E. Niebauer, A. Delorme, L. Carpenter, D. Radin, and G. Yount. 2020. "A Case Study of Extended Human Capacity Perception During Energy Medicine Treatments Using Mixed-Methods Analysis." *Explore* (October): S1550830720303542. https://doi.org/10.1016/j.explore.2020.10.006

Wahbeh, H., and D. Radin. 2018. "People Reporting Experiences of Mediumship Have Higher Dissociation Symptom Scores than Non-Mediums, but Below Thresholds for Pathological Dissociation [Version 3; Referees: 2 Approved, 1 Not Approved]." *F1000Research* 6, no. 1416.

Wahbeh, H., D. Radin, J. Mossbridge, C. Vieten, and A. Delorme. 2018. "Exceptional Experiences Reported by Scientists and Engineers." *Explore* 14, no. 5: 329–341. https://doi.org/10.1016/j.explore.2018.05.002

Wahbeh, H., D. Radin, G. Yount, M. A. Woodley, M. A. Sarraf, and M. V. Karpuj. 2021. "Genetics of Psychic Ability: A Pilot Case-Control Exome Sequencing Study." *Explore*. In press.

Wahbeh, H., A. Sagher, W. Back, P. Pundhir, and F. Travis. 2018. "A Systematic Review of Transcendent States Across Meditation and Contemplative Traditions." *Explore* 14, no. 1: 19–35. https://doi.org/10.1016/j.explore.2017.07.007

Wahbeh, H., G. Yount, C. Vieten, D. Radin, and A. Delorme. 2020. "Measuring Extraordinary Experiences and Beliefs: A Validation and Reliability Study [Version 3; Peer Review: 3 Approved]." *F1000Research* 8, no. 1741: 29. https://doi.org/10.12688/f1000research.20409.3

Waller, N. G., and C. A. Ross. 1997. "The Prevalence and Biometric Structure of Pathological Dissociation in the General Population: Taxometric and Behavior Genetic Findings." *Journal of Abnormal Psychology* 106, no. 4: 499–510.

Waller, N. G., F. W. Putnam, and E. B. Carlson. 1996. "Types of Dissociation and Dissociative Types: A Taxometric Analysis of Dissociative Experiences." *Psychological Methods* 1, no. 3: 300.

White, R. A. 1994. "Exceptional Human Experience and the More We Are: Exceptional Human Experience and Identity." In Proceedings of the Academy of Religion and Psychical research Annual Conferences, 75: 1–13.

Wright, D. B., and E. F. Loftus. 1999. "Measuring Dissociation: Comparison of Alternative Forms of the Dissociative Experiences Scale." *The American Journal of Psychology* 112, no. 4: 497. https://doi.org/10.2307/1423648

Wulff, D. M. 2000. "Mystical Experience." In *Varieties of Anomalous Experience: Examining the Scientific Evidence*. Washington, DC: American Psychological Association.

Yao, X-C, T-X Wang, P. Xu, H. Lu, G-S Pan, X-H Bao, C-Z Peng, C-Y Lu, Y-A Chen, and J-W Pan. 2012. "Observation of Eight-Photon Entanglement." *Nature Photonics* 6, no. 4: 225–228.

Yount, G., A. Delorme, D. Radin, L. Carpenter, J. Anastasia, M. Pierson, S. Steele, H. Mandell, A. Chagnon, and H. Wahbeh. 2021. "Energy Medicine Treatments for Hand and Wrist Pain: A Pilot Study." *Explore*. In press.

Zander, T., M. Ollinger, and K. G. Volz. 2016. "Intuition and Insight: Two Processes That Build on Each Other or Fundamentally Differ?" *Frontiers in Psychology* 7: 1395. https://doi.org/10.3389/fpsyg.2016.01395

Endnotes

1   My great-uncle, who was an Orthodox Christian priest, would regularly do house clearings and exorcisms throughout his life. My grandfather continued this work with his book *Life After Death* and regular "meetings." My uncle Zaher collated all of his automatic writings into a book called *From a Gun to a Flower.*

2   Applied kinesiology is used widely by chiropractors and other health professionals around the world (http://www.icakusa.com/). A related method, electroacupuncture according to Voll (Vega), uses the energy meridian system to evaluate what strengthens or weakens the body (https://www.researchgate.net/publication/290437736_Electroacupuncture _According_to_Voll_Historical_Background_and_Literature_Review.) Both of these methods have mixed reviews for their efficacy in diagnosing illnesses, but many clinicians find clear improvements in their patients in using these techniques.

3   Anomalous cognition refers to the apparent reception of information in ways that are currently unexplained, anomalous perturbation refers to the seeming influence of mind on matter (such as psychokinetic effects on microscopic systems) in ways that are currently unexplained, and anomalous force refers to psychokinesis one can see with the naked eye. Parapsychologist Rhea White, who contributed a great deal to the field, coined her own term, "exceptional human experiences," in the 1990s, which included psychic, mystical, encounter-type experiences, and death-related experiences highlighting people's subjective experience of them.

4   The goal of this book is to give an overview for the layperson and so may gloss over nuances for the science-minded reader. The references are included so you can go more deeply into the complexity of the topics presented.

5   A conservative clinical cutoff for the DES-T is a score higher than 20, although this threshold continues to be debated (Waller and Ross 1997; Leavitt 1999; Wright and Loftus 1999).

6   Forced-choice tasks can use between two and six options for the correct
     answer, and the options can be pictures, symbols, letters, shapes, etc.
     Forced-choice, in which the target-guess is "one of a limited range of
     possibilities which are known to [the participant] in advance," is different
     from free-choice, which "describes any test of ESP [extrasensory
     perception] in which the range of possible targets is relatively unlimited
     and is unknown to the percipient" (Thalbourne 2003, 44).

7   Laboratory tasks other than the forced-choice task have not shown the
     same clear relationship with belief (Hitchman, Roe, and Sherwood 2012).
     The effect of belief on performance may depend on the specific task
     (Cardeña, Palmer, and Marcusson-Clavertz 2015).

8   Telepathy: "felt as though you were in touch with someone when they
     were far away from you"; clairvoyance: "seen events that happened at a
     great distance as they were happening"; contact with the dead: "felt as
     though you were really in touch with someone who died."

9   "Extended human capacities" is the term I usually start out with if I'm
     not sure of people's openness to channeling. If the person doesn't know
     what that is, I can explain the types of experiences that includes.

10   While meta-analyses are usually thought of as the top of the hierarchy
     of evidence pyramid, there are some critiques of meta-analyses in the
     field (Bierman, Spottiswoode, and Bijl 2016).

11   There is some contention about these results and experimenter effects
     in this body of research. See Varvoglis and Bancel 2015 for an excellent
     review of these issues.

12   Some have suggested alternative models of explanation for these effects
     than the influence of collective consciousness—namely, goal-oriented
     effects of the investigator, methodological errors or leaks that bias the
     formal replications, conventional perturbations of RNG output due to
     ambient electromagnetic fields, or a fortuitous selection of events and
     parameters through experimenter intuition and retroactive information
     (Bancel 2017; Varvoglis and Bancel 2015).

13   The effect size for remote staring was 0.128. The NEMO Science Center
     in Amsterdam boasts the largest experiment study on the sense of
     being stared at, with over eighteen thousand pairs of people and highly
     significant positive results.

14 This paradigm was called attention-focusing facilitation studies, initiated by Dr. William Braud and replicated by other researchers.

15 William Braud pioneered DMILS, or direct mental interactions with living systems, in 1977, launching numerous studies by himself and others where pairs of people were studied to evaluate the changes in physiology from intention.

16 Different physiological measures have been shown to change, like signals from the skin (electrodermal activity), blood volume, activation of different parts of the brain (functional magnetic resonance imaging [fMRI]; Achterberg et al. 2005), brain waves (EEG; Richards et al. 2005), and heart rate. To date, there have been three meta-analyses, or analyses that synthesize multiple studies looking at the same measurements, for DMILS paradigm studies (Schmidt 2012, 2015; Schmidt et al. 2004).

17 The most recent meta-analysis at the time of this writing was conducted by Dr. Stefan Schmidt (Schmidt et al. 2004). It included thirty-six studies and found an effect size of 0.106. Effect sizes give a quantitative measure of how much our experimental condition influenced our variable of interest. Common convention for Cohen's d effects sizes are as follows: $d=0.2$ "small" effect size, $d=0.5$ "medium" effect size, and $d=0.8$ a "large" effect size. We would expect an effect size of 0 if the channeling phenomena studied were not real.

18 The study was a meta-analysis of fifty-seven studies. The effect size for noncontact healing studies was 0.203 for all human studies, and 0.224 for the twenty-seven studies of the fifty-seven that were high quality; 0.25 for in-vitro studies, 0.25 for nonhuman animal studies, and 0.2 for plant studies, all statistically significant.

19 While Star Gate found evidence for remote viewing, or what they call informational psi, they did not find evidence for psychokinesis or causal psi.

20 Effect sizes range from 0.17 to 0.39. These are the strongest we've seen in parapsychology research. Some clinical trials for meditation and other mind-body or behavioral interventions in psychology reach these levels and are considered positive trials.

21 See International Remote Viewing Association (http://www.irva.org) for more information about remote viewing, and Soul Rider (https://thesoul rider.net) for more information of using remote viewing for financial purposes.

22   The effect size for the experiments was 0.20 for the complete database and 0.24 for independent replications, which is very similar to Dr. Bem's original experiment, which had an effect size of 0.22.

23   For an excellent review of mental mediumship, see Beischel and Zingrone 2015.

24   See http://www.challengercc.org/.

25   For more, greater detail of some of these theories and their relationship to parapsychology, see Millar 2015, Cardeña 2018, and Stanford 2015. There are many more resources for these concepts, but these are a good place to start.

26   For an excellent review of psychedelics and channeling experiences, see Luke 2012 and 2015.

27   See https://www.chi.is/.

28   The transcripts of this channeling are available upon request.

29   I had forgotten about the pineal gland being called the "seat of the soul" until this channeling. That is what led me to look up the literature on the pineal gland and channeling.

30   They went on to mention possession-type experiences: "Now, we know that there are instances when this happens, when there is not consent and the spirit will take over without permission and as higher beings. This is against our ethics and is not done. However, we do know that you are aware of such instances. And so in this way, it is not a synchronization of the spirit with the channeler's vital force, but a co-opting, if you will. But we know that your book is not focused on those types of experiences, so we will go back to the other examples."

31   Openness measures a person's willingness to try new things, be comfortable with new things, and even enjoy new things. People with high openness scores are also creative and enjoy a variety of things in their lives. People score high in conscientiousness when they are reliable and impeccable, organized and thorough. Extraversion measures a person's enjoyment of connecting with others and being talkative, assertive, and outgoing. Agreeableness measures a person's easy-going nature and their friendliness, cooperative tendencies, affection, and compassion. Neuroticism measures a person's emotional stability and how much negative emotions they experience.

32 For a great discussion about capacity, ability, and skill, see Braude 2003.

33 Kardecism or Spiritism is a spiritualist philosophy started by Hippolyte Léon Denizard Rivail under the pen name Allen Kardec in the 1800s. The communication with nonphysical beings was a central practice in this tradition.

34 These are housed at the Missouri Historical Society in St. Louis.

35 For a wonderfully thorough examination of the case of Patience Worth, see chapter 5 of Stephan Braude's *Immortal Remains* (Braude 2003, 133–175).

36 Stephen Braude gives a great description of what he calls the usual and unusual suspects (Braude 2003, 10–11). The usual suspects include fraud, reporting incorrect information, or observing incorrect information. Yes, unfortunately there are some people who claim to be mediums that are purposefully faking the information. Dr. Braude also mentions other more unusual sources of information that comes from mediumistic communication. One is mental illness of dissociative disorders that we talked about in chapter 2. The other is that some people may have exceptional memories, extraordinary skill or brilliance in some limited field, or rare creative talents that are undeveloped or hidden.

37 See Braude 2003 and Kean 2018 and *Is There Life After Death?* published by the Society of Psychical Research.

38 See Roberto Assagioli's work on psychosynthesis (https://www.aap-psycho synthesis.org/What-is-Psychosynthesis).

Helané Wahbeh, ND, MCR, is director of research at the Institute of Noetic Sciences (IONS). She is clinically trained as a naturopathic physician, and research-trained with a master's of clinical research and two postdoctoral research fellowships. Her research domains include extended human capacities, complementary and alternative medicine, mind-body medicine, stress, and post-traumatic stress disorder (PTSD).

Foreword writer **Eben Alexander, MD**, spent more than twenty-five years as an academic neurosurgeon, including fifteen years at the Brigham and Women's Hospital, the Children's Hospital, and Harvard Medical School in Boston, MA. He is author of *Proof of Heaven*, a *New York Times* bestseller.

The Institute of Noetic Sciences

The Institute of Noetic Sciences (IONS) is a research center and direct-experience lab specializing in the intersection of science and profound human experience.

For centuries, the power of science has unlocked the mysteries of the natural world and driven human innovation. As Dr. Edgar Mitchell returned to Earth from his moonwalk on Apollo 14, he had a profound transcendence experience that led him to establish IONS in 1973. He understood that by applying the scientific rigor used in his explorations of outer space, we could better understand the mysteries of inner space—the space in which he felt an undeniable sense of interconnection and oneness. The mission of IONS is to reveal the interconnected nature of reality through scientific exploration and personal discovery, creating a more compassionate, thriving, and sustainable world.

At IONS, we are inspired by the power of science to explain phenomena not previously understood, harnessing the best of the rational mind to make advances that further our knowledge and deepen our knowing. For over four decades, IONS has provided a safe harbor for scientists and scholars to pursue research into frontier questions related to the nature of consciousness, and for healers and educators to work with emerging ideas. From our scientific exploration, we design experiential programs for personal discovery that allow each of us to access more of our human capacities and the fullness of our humanity.

Today, IONS continues to forge new frontiers in consciousness research and experiential education, developing training programs for youth, adults, elders, and professionals; all on a majestic 197-acre retreat center in Petaluma, CA, one hour north of San Francisco, CA.

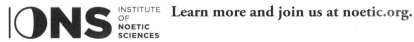

IONS INSTITUTE OF NOETIC SCIENCES **Learn more and join us at noetic.org.**

MORE BOOKS for the SPIRITUAL SEEKER

ISBN: 978-1684035021 | US $21.95

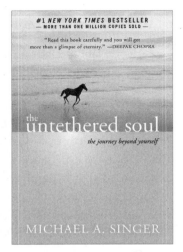

ISBN: 978-1572245372 | US $18.95

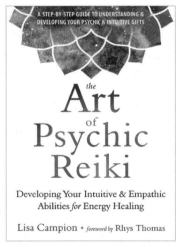

ISBN: 978-1684031214 | US $19.95

ISBN: 978-1684035724 | US $18.95

newharbingerpublications

NON-DUALITY PRESS | REVEAL PRESS